D

PRA
FAS

> ractical, powerful and proven ... ...ging risk in
> any organisation.

Peter Ward, Retired Financial Services Partner, AT Kearney and KPMG

> Keith Baxter's book is a must-read for every business executive.
> The ABCD approach cuts through the normal risk hype and
> techno-speak. A complex subject brought down to basics – coloured
> bubbles are simple and easy to understand.

David Spinks, Operational Risk Manager,
HP Enterprise Services

> Genuinely startling insight into communicating and managing
> risk.

Paul Hamilton, Chief Executive, Business Enterprise Solutions, Abu Dhabi

> Keith has been a real authority on risk management, long
> before it became as topical as it is today. That knowledge really
> shows in this book.

Steve Young, Managing Director of IndeGo Consulting

> Essential reading for project managers and anyone involved
> in large and complex projects. This book addresses the
> problems that have haunted risk management for years. Based on my
> experience, the ABCD process really does identify the risks that other risk
> processes leave behind.

Terry McKenna MBA MProjMgt PMP, Founder and Managing Consultant at
www.startprojectmanagement.com

FAST TRACK TO SUCCESS

RISK
MANAGEMENT

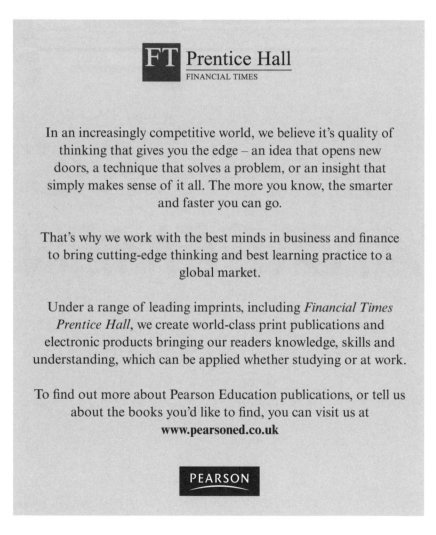

FT Prentice Hall
FINANCIAL TIMES

In an increasingly competitive world, we believe it's quality of thinking that gives you the edge – an idea that opens new doors, a technique that solves a problem, or an insight that simply makes sense of it all. The more you know, the smarter and faster you can go.

That's why we work with the best minds in business and finance to bring cutting-edge thinking and best learning practice to a global market.

Under a range of leading imprints, including *Financial Times Prentice Hall*, we create world-class print publications and electronic products bringing our readers knowledge, skills and understanding, which can be applied whether studying or at work.

To find out more about Pearson Education publications, or tell us about the books you'd like to find, you can visit us at **www.pearsoned.co.uk**

PEARSON

FAST TRACK TO SUCCESS

RISK
MANAGEMENT

KEITH BAXTER

**Financial Times
Prentice Hall
is an imprint of**

Harlow, England • London • New York • Boston • San Francisco • Toronto • Sydney • Singapore • Hong Kong
Tokyo • Seoul • Taipei • New Delhi • Cape Town • Madrid • Mexico City • Amsterdam • Munich • Paris • Milan

PEARSON EDUCATION LIMITED

Edinburgh Gate
Harlow CM20 2JE
Tel: +44 (0)1279 623623
Fax: +44 (0)1279 431059
Website: www.pearsoned.co.uk

First published in Great Britain in 2010

ISBN: 978-0-273-73286-0

British Library Cataloguing-in-Publication Data
A catalogue record for this book is available from the British Library

Library of Congress Cataloging-in-Publication Data
Baxter, Keith, 1959–
    Fast track to success : risk management / Keith Baxter. -- 1st ed.
        p. cm.
    Includes index.
    ISBN 978-0-273-73286-0 (pbk.)
    1. Risk management. I. Title.
    HD61.B398 2010
    658.15'5--dc22

                                                          2010026324

10 9 8 7 6 5 4 3 2 1
14 13 12 11 10

Series text design by Design Deluxe

Typeset in 10/15 Swis Lt by 30
Printed and bound in Great Britain by Ashford Colour Press, Gosport

CONTENTS

The Fast Track way ix

About the author xii

A word of thanks from the author xiii

Risk management Fast Track xv

How to use this book xix

Fast-Track-Me.com xx

A AWARENESS 1
  1 Risk management in a nutshell 5
  2 Risk management process audit 21

B BUSINESS FAST TRACK 31
  3 Fast Track top ten 35
  4 Technologies 99
  5 Implementing change 113

C CAREER FAST TRACK 127
  6 The first ten weeks 131
  7 Leading the team 151
  8 Getting to the top 169

D DIRECTOR'S TOOLKIT 185
  T1 Assessing the risk management maturity of the organisation 189
  T2 Accurately quantifying risk 195
  T3 Using risk as a competitive differentiator 201
  T4 Black Swans – avoiding business disasters 207

The Fast Track way 213

Other titles in the Fast Track series 215

Glossary 216

Index 219

THE FAST TRACK WAY

Everything you need to accelerate your career

The best way to fast track your career as a manager is to fast track the contribution you and your team make to your organisation and for your team to be successful in as public a way as possible. That's what the Fast Track series is about. The Fast Track manager delivers against performance expectations, is personally highly effective and efficient, develops the full potential of their team, is recognised as a key opinion leader in the business, and ultimately progresses up the organisation ahead of their peers.

You will benefit from the books in the Fast Track series whether you are an ambitious first-time team leader or a more experienced manager who is keen to develop further over the next few years. You may be a specialist aiming to master every aspect of your chosen discipline or function, or simply be trying to broaden your awareness of other key management disciplines and skills. In either case, you will have the motivation to critically review yourself and your team using the tools and techniques presented in this book, as well as the time to stop, think and act on areas you identify for improvement.

Do you know what you need to know and do to make a real difference to your performance at work, your contribution to your company and your blossoming career? For most of us, the honest answer is 'Not really, no'. It's not surprising then that most of us never reach our full potential. The innovative Fast Track series gives you exactly what you need to speed up your progress and become a high performance manager in all the areas of the business that matter. Fast Track is not just another 'How to' series. Books on selling tell you how to win sales but not how to move from salesperson to sales manager. Project management software enables you to plan detailed tasks but doesn't improve the quality of your project management thinking and business performance. A marketing book tells you about the principles of marketing but not how to lead a team of marketers. It's not enough.

Specially designed features in the Fast Track books will help you to see what you need to know and to develop the skills you need to be successful. They give you:

→ the information required for you to shine in your chosen function or skill – particularly in the Fast Track top ten;

→ practical advice in the form of Quick Tips and answers to FAQs from people who have been there before you and succeeded;

→ state of the art best practice as explained by today's academics and industry experts in specially written Expert Voices;

→ case stories and examples of what works and, perhaps more importantly, what doesn't work;

→ comprehensive tools for accelerating the effectiveness and performance of your team;

→ a framework that helps you to develop your career as well as produce terrific results.

Fast Track is a resource of business thinking, approaches and techniques presented in a variety of ways – in short, a complete performance support environment. It enables managers to build careers from their first tentative steps into management all the way up to becoming a business director – accelerating the performance of their team and their career. When you use the Fast Track approach with your team it provides a common business language and structure, based on best business practice. You will benefit from the book whether or not others in the organisation adopt the same practices; indeed if they don't, it will give you an edge over them. Each Fast Track book blends hard practical advice from expert practitioners with insights and the latest thinking from experts from leading business schools.

The Fast Track approach will be valuable to team leaders and managers from all industry sectors and functional areas. It is for ambitious people who have already acquired some team leadership skills and have realised just how much more there is to know.

If you want to progress further you will be directed towards additional learning and development resources via an interactive Fast Track website, **www.Fast-Track-Me.com**. For many, these books therefore become the first step in a journey of continuous development. So, the Fast Track approach gives you everything you need to accelerate your career, offering you the opportunity to develop your knowledge and skills, improve your team's performance, benefit your organisation's progress towards its aims and light the fuse under your true career potential.

ABOUT THE AUTHOR

KEITH BAXTER is an internationally renowned risk management expert who has specialised in the field for over 20 years.

In the early part of his career, Keith worked on a number of very large defence programmes that all went very wrong. Intrigued by the management failures that seemed to happen repeatedly, he started to focus on how risk management could avoid these disasters. However, his frustration with traditional risk management approaches led to the development of the ABCD risk management process and associated tools.

In the 1990s, with the management consultants AT Kearney, Keith applied ABCD-based techniques to virtually every industry and on every continent (apart from Antarctica). In 2000, Keith founded De-RISK as an organisation that provides Enterprise Risk Management solutions based on the ABCD process and Assure web-based toolset.

A regular on the risk management conference circuit and frequently published in leading journals, this is his first book and the first book to be published that covers the ABCD methodology.

For recreation he likes to apply risk management to a variety of risky pursuits that tend to involve climbing up or riding down mountains.

E   kbaxter@de-risk.com

W www.de-risk.com

W www.linkedin.com/in/keithbaxter

W http://twitter.com/De_Risky

A WORD OF THANKS
FROM THE AUTHOR

I would like to thank the following for their generous contributions to this book.

→ **Liz Gooster, Pearson.** There are many exciting new ideas in the publishing world at present, but without an enthusiastic champion, most will simply die a slow death. Liz had the confidence to commission the Fast Track series and associated web-tool on behalf of the Pearson Group at a time when other publishers were cutting back on non-core activities. She has remained committed to its success – providing direction, challenge and encouragement as and when required.

→ **Ken Langdon.** As well as being a leading author in his own right, Ken has worked with all the Fast Track authors to bring a degree of rigour and consistency to the series. As each book has developed, he has been a driving force behind the scenes, pulling the detailed content for each title together in the background – working with an equal measure of enthusiasm and patience!

→ **Mollie Dickenson.** Mollie has a background in publishing and works as a research manager at Henley Business School, and has been a supporter of the project from its inception. She has provided constant encouragement and challenge, and is, as always, an absolute delight to work with.

→ **Critical readers.** As the Fast Track series evolved, it was vital that we received constant challenge and input from other experts and from critical readers.

→ **Professor David Birchall.** David has worked to identify and source Expert Voice contributions from international academic and business experts in each Fast Track title. David is co-author of the Fast Track *Innovation* book and a leading academic author in his own right, and has spent much of the last 20 years heading up the research programme at Henley Business School – one of the world's top ten business schools.

Our expert team

Last but not least, I am grateful for the contributions made by experts from around the world in each of the Fast Track titles.

EXPERT	TOPIC	BUSINESS SCHOOL/ COMPANY
Professor Steve Tippins	Risk managers and the future (p. 19)	Roosevelt University, LA Crosse, Wisconsin, Canada
Dr Steve Simister	Risk management standards and processes (p. 28)	Henley Business School, University of Reading
Professor Chris Chapman	Clarifying the 'risk' in risk management (p. 96)	Emeritus Professor, University of Southampton, School of Management
Professor Giampiero Favato	Real options and scenario planning: an integrated approach to investment risk management (p. 109)	Kingston Business School, London
Professor Stephen Ward	Operational risk and infrastructure (p. 123)	University of Southampton, School of Management
Professor Petter Gottschalk	Intelligence sources in risk management (p. 146)	Norwegian School of Management
Professor Giampiero Favato	Parametric cost analysis improves the quality of stop–go decisions in pharmaceutical R&D (p. 166)	Kingston Business School, London
Dr Whitney van der Linde	Risk management: a business enabler (p. 182)	Department of Business and Management, University of Johannesburg, SA

RISK MANAGEMENT FAST TRACK

Risk management is probably one of the hottest topics of today, but why? Most industries are now highly competitive and the generic mantra is: better, faster, cheaper. With these pressures comes risk – lots of it. If the risk is not managed the results are poor, slow and expensive. Managing risks, and, of conversely taking opportunities, will have a big impact on both the bottom and the top line of your business.

Risk management was heading up the business agenda but the financial crisis of the late noughties pushed it right to the top. Most people agree that the root cause of the crisis was a failure of risk management in some shape or form. With this added focus, most organisations are prioritising risk management higher, and risk management roles are valued more highly and rewarded appropriately.

However, this is only the tip of the iceberg as risk management should be a core capability for every individual in the organisation. From the board members who need to understand how to set risk strategy, to operational managers who should understand how to protect the ongoing business, and project managers who need to understand how to systematically deliver objectives within time and budget constraints. Risk management should be part of their DNA.

The problem is that most business people think that they understand how to 'do' risk management. Most organisations have audit driven risk management procedures that encourage people to 'tick the boxes', and we saw how ineffective they were in the past few years. The concepts of risk management are indeed simple but the effective application is not and this is where the Risk Management FastTrack is targeted.

One useful model – see the figure opposite – that may help to get us started is the **six 'Ps'** that companies that manage risks successfully tend to get right: planning, prioritisation, process, platform, people and performance. All are elements of an integrated framework – like a chain, it's only as strong as its weakest link.

Taking the six Ps in order, **planning** reflects the fact that every venture needs to start with strategy. Over the next few years, what are the high-growth or high-revenue areas the CEO wants the company to focus on? What are the success factors something new will need to take into account? For a fizzy drink supplier, for example, an obvious strategic driver would be the trend towards healthy drinking. Planning therefore provides a context for the risks and ensures that the strategic risks are considered early and appropriately. Without plans, what is the risk related to?

Prioritisation is everywhere in risk management. You need to prioritise the business areas, the programmes in the business, then the projects within the programmes and also the ongoing business processes. This is key as you must focus on the most critical and complex ventures if you want to identify the biggest risks. Finally, the risks within each venture must also be prioritised to make sure that valuable resources are focused on the right risks at the right time.

Process is the way in which risks are identified, analysed and managed. A great failing with traditional approaches in risk management is the lack of process: for example, risks do not identify themselves and if you use simple forms to capture risks or unstructured workshops you are likely to end up with a lot of noise and a lot of manual work to rescue any value from the exercise.

Platform refers to the software tools that you use to capture, analyse, manipulate and report on risks. This could be a simple spreadsheet but any serious venture is going need a web-based tool that allows easy access to information and facilitates the communication of risk around the organisation. Also, a web-based tool gives senior managers visibility, control and confidence over the entire risk management process and content. The software also ensures that all teams follow a common approach based on best practice, and provides the status reports needed at the regular risk review meetings.

The risk management process and tools will only be effective if the right **people** are engaged at the right level and the right time. This should start with an executive sponsor who acts as the risk process champion and sells the benefits of the process to management whenever appropriate. The risk manager controls and provides the focal point for the risk management process. Finally, the risk team members (if appropriate) who need a combination of business skills and interpersonal skills to ensure that the right information is captured from management/team members. Just as important is the risk attitude of the management and team members who need to 'think risk' by being open to the concepts of risk management and understand and support the risk process.

Performance, the final P, drives all of this. It is very difficult to measure the effectiveness of risk management due to its probabilistic nature: for example, you can take specific mitigating actions but the risk might not have happened even if you had done nothing. It is therefore important to measure the effectiveness of the process by measuring metrics related to action follow-through and reward appropriate risk behaviour to create a virtuous circle of continuous improvement. The improvement in business performance due to risk management should then be clear.

Risk management is a crucial part of ensuring business performance. Too often, today's managers are fixated by the company's profit and loss statements, the information that impresses actual or prospective shareholders. But financial reports tend to focus on past performance, which we liken to trying to drive a car by looking in the rear-view mirror. Whilst keeping an eye on the current financials is important, future success depends on looking ahead for the risks that are on or just over the horizon and taking appropriate proactive actions to avoid disasters and keep your business ahead of the competition.

Risk management needs champions, people who will drive through the problems and setbacks, convince sceptics of the need for formal risk management and believe that the process will ultimately deliver. Perhaps you are that champion: perhaps just for your team, project or division of your company, or perhaps for the entire organisation as the chief risk officer. Whatever your aspirations, you have an exciting time ahead. There will always be risks and it's your job to identify, prioritise and manage them. That's a big job, so let's get on with it.

HOW TO USE THIS BOOK

Fast Track books present a collection of the latest tools, techniques and advice to help build your team and your career. Use this table to plan your route through the book.

PART	OVERVIEW
About the authors	A brief overview of the authors, their background and their contact details
A **Awareness**	*This first part gives you an opportunity to gain a quick overview of the topic and to reflect on your current effectiveness*
1 *Risk management in a nutshell*	A brief overview of risk management and a series of frequently asked questions to bring you up to speed quickly
2 *Risk management process audit*	Simple checklists to help identify strengths and weaknesses in your team and your capabilities
B **Business Fast Track**	*Part B provides tools and techniques that may form part of the integrated risk management framework for you and your team*
3 *Fast Track top ten*	Ten tools and techniques used to help you implement a sustainable approach to risk management based on the latest best practice
4 *Technologies*	A review of the latest information technologies used to improve effectiveness and efficiency of risk management activities
5 *Implementing change*	A detailed checklist to identify gaps and to plan the changes necessary to implement your risk management improvements
C **Career Fast Track**	*Part C focuses on you, your leadership qualities and what it takes to get to the top*
6 *The first ten weeks*	Recommended activities when starting a new role in risk management, together with a checklist of useful facts to know
7 *Leading the team*	Managing change, building your team and deciding your leadership style
8 *Getting to the top*	Becoming a risk management professional, getting promoted and becoming a director – what does it take?
D **Director's toolkit**	*The final part provides more advanced tools and techniques based on industry best practice*
Toolkit	Advanced risk tools and techniques used by senior managers
Glossary	Glossary of terms

FAST-TRACK-ME.COM

Before reading this book, why not start by visiting our companion website **www.Fast-Track-Me.com**? This is a custom-designed, highly interactive online resource that addresses the needs of the busy manager by providing access to ideas and methods that will

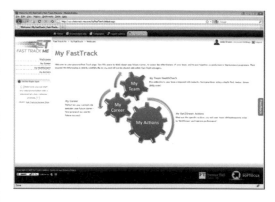

improve individual and team performance quickly, and develop both your skills and your career.

As well as giving you access to cutting-edge business knowledge across a range of key topics – including the subject of this book – **Fast-Track-Me.com** will enable you to stop and think about what you want to achieve in your chosen career and where you want to take your team. By doing this, it will provide a context for reading and give you extra information and access to a range of interactive features.

The site in general is packed with valuable features, such as:

→ **The Knowledge Cube**. The K-Cube is a two-dimensional matrix presenting Fast Track features from all topics in a consistent and easy-to-use way – providing ideas, tools and techniques in a single place, anytime, anywhere. This is a great way to delve in and out of business topics quickly.

→ **The Online Coach**. The Online Coach is a toolkit of fully inter-active business templates in MS Word format that allow Fast-Track-Me.com users to explore specific business methods (strategy, ideas, projects etc.) and learn from concepts, case examples and other resources according to your preferred learning style.

→ **Business Glossary**. The Fast Track Business Glossary pro-vides a comprehensive list of key words associated with each title in the Fast Track series together with a plain English defini-tion – helping you to cut through business jargon.

To access even more features, carry out self-diagnostic tests and develop your own personal profile, simply log-in and register – then click on My FastTrack to get started! Give yourself the Fast Track Health Check now.

My FastTrack

These are the different areas you'll discover in the My FastTrack area.

My HealthCheck

How effective is your team compared with industry 'best practices'? Find out using a simple Red, Amber, Green (RAG) scale.

After identifying areas of concern, you can plan for their resolution using a personal 'Get2Green' action plan.

My Get2Green Actions

What are the specific actions you and your team will implement in order to 'Get2Green' and improve performance? Log, prioritise and monitor your action points in the My Get2Green Action Plan area to help you plan for future success – fast.

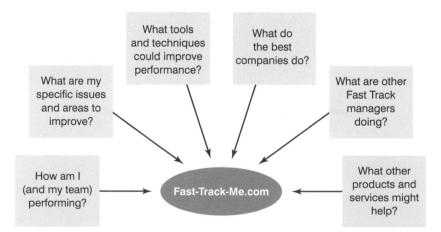

My Career

Reflect on your current role and plan your future career – how prepared are you for future success?

Fast-Track-Me.com provides the busy manager with access to the latest thinking, techniques and tools at their fingertips. It can also help answer some of the vital questions managers are asking themselves today.

What tools and techniques could improve performance?

What do the best companies do?

What are my specific issues and areas to improve?

What are other Fast Track managers doing?

How am I (and my team) performing?

Fast-Track-Me.com

What other products and services might help?

Don't get left behind: log on to **www.Fast-Track-Me.com** now to get your career on the fast track.

AWARENESS

This book introduces a sustainable approach to risk management aimed at keeping you, your team and your organisation at the forefront of risk management, thus contributing towards the future of all three. The starting point is to gain a quick understanding of what risk management is and what it is not, and to be aware of your own and your team's capabilities in this area right now. For this reason we will ask you a number of questions that will reveal where you and your team need to improve if you are to have a mature approach to risk management in your business.

'Know yourself' was the motto above the doorway of the Oracle at Delphi and is a wise thought. It means that you must do an open and honest self-audit as you start on the process of setting up your framework for risk management.

The stakes are high. Risk management is at the heart of success in this global, competitive marketplace. Your team therefore, need to be effective risk managers and you need to be a good leader in risk management. Poor leadership and poor team effectiveness will make failure likely. An effective team poorly led will sap the team's energy and lead in the long term to failure through their leaving for a better environment or becoming less effective through lack of motivation. Leading an ineffective team well does not prevent the obvious conclusion that an ineffective team will not thrive. So, looking at the figure below, how do you make sure that you and your team are in the top right-hand box – an innovative and effective team with an excellent leader? That's what this book is about and this part shows you how to discover your and your team's starting point.

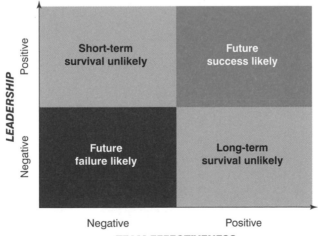

RISK MANAGEMENT IN A NUTSHELL

Starting with the basics

Just what is risk management?

The term 'risk management' can mean many different things to different people. To some the phrase is exciting – it's all about taking and managing risks. To others the phrase is a big turn-off – it reeks of control and bureaucracy. However you look at it, in a world of uncertainty, risk is inevitable and actually desirable. If we had no uncertainty and therefore no risk, then life, including business life, would be predictable, unrewarding and boring.

So maybe the term risk management needs to be dissected. Risk is 'exciting' but management is 'boring'? But risk taking without management is reckless and we all know many (recent) examples of that. In everyday life as in business specifically, all risk takers are good risk managers or they end up dead – metaphorically or literally.

Risk management is also a term that means different things to different businesses. In banking and insurance, risk management tends to be a purely financial process for measuring (and hopefully managing) financial exposure. To the manager of a nuclear power plant, risk management is all about avoiding physical disaster. To the manager of a large change project, it's making sure that delivery is on time, within budget and the project meets its objectives.

Trying to be a little more structured about this, without trying to be exhaustive, the main areas of risk management are:

→ **Financial risk management**: the process of evaluating and managing current and possible financial risk in a business in order to decrease the business's exposure to the risk. Financial risk managers must identify the risk, evaluate all possible remedies and then implement steps necessary to alleviate the risk. These risks are typically analysed by using financial instruments such as indicators, losses, scenario analysis, stress testing and mathematical modelling as a method of counteracting possible ramifications. Financial risk management tends to concentrate on credit risk and market risk. Financial risk management cannot protect a firm from all possible risks because some are unexpected and cannot be addressed quickly enough. All financial intuitions have significant risk management functions and large corporations have scaled-down risk management departments normally as part of their audit or treasury functions.

→ **Insurance**: the promise of covering the risk of potential future losses in exchange for a periodic payment. Insurance is designed to protect the financial well-being of an individual, company or other entity in the case of unexpected loss. Agreeing to the terms of an insurance policy creates a contract between the insured and the insurer. In exchange for payments from the insured (i.e. the premiums), the insurer agrees to pay the policyholder a sum of money upon the occurrence of a specific event. The classic example of insurance is in the shipping industry where ships and their cargoes are covered by policies which pay out if the worst risks are realised.

→ **Operational risk management**: the management of the non-(purely) financial aspects of the business. This focuses on the risk to the ongoing business processes and the potential for them to break down. For example, the risk of fraud in a bank's payment system could lead to major unchecked losses, or the fire in a data centre could lead to serious breakdown of business continuity. This would also cover the reputational risk to the organisation if a process or product fails.

→ **Programme/project risk management**: the management of the deliverables of a programme or project designed to initiate some kind of change to the business. This could be a new product development, a new IT system or a business process re-engineering. The risks are always focused on cost overruns, delays to plans and compromised objectives. This would also include the reputational risk to the business if the project fails to deliver to planned expectations, for example the overrun (timescales and/or budget) of a major new sporting facility.

Risk management in banking and financial terms is a mature process that is effective, if it is followed, and there are many books on this subject – this is not one of them. This is a book that aims to address 'enterprise risk management', i.e. the total risk to the enterprise or business but without trying to add to the body of knowledge that is traditional financial risk management. Instead we will concentrate on the areas of risk management that are the most difficult to define, develop and deliver but often yield the most benefit. This is often called 'operational risk management' but it really covers all aspects of enterprise risk that are not purely financial. In particular, the area of risk management that is the most difficult and underdeveloped in practice is project or programme risk management and this is a central focus of this book.

Traditional risk management

As our starting point I will summarise risk management as it is traditionally practised in most organisations. Again we are not looking at established financial risk management techniques but more the operational risk management that, in many businesses, will also include project risk management. You need to understand the overall traditional risk management process but I will ultimately recommend that you don't follow it in a traditional way – read on and all will be revealed.

Risk management is basically composed of risk assessment (passive) and risk control (active) and breaks down into the following six stages that relate to the figure overleaf:

1 **Identify** your risks: common methods to identify risks are workshops, brainstorming and distributing standard templates for team members to complete.

2 Analyse: traditionally you do this by allocating numbers or ratings to describe 'impact' and 'probability'. Impact is normally described quantitatively, in terms of financial loss if the risk occurs, or qualitatively by using a high/medium/low (HML) type scale. Probability is normally expressed as a percentage likelihood that the risk will occur (if no action is taken) but may also be allocated a HML type scale.

3 Prioritise: normally done by multiplying together the impact and probability to come up with a 'risk exposure'. This will either be a number or a HML type scale as before. Risks are then normally prioritised from highest to lowest risk exposure.

4 Risk management planning: this involves deciding on your objectives for managing the risk: for example, do we mitigate the risk, accept it, transfer it, insure against it and so on?

5 Risk mitigation/resolution: breaking down the risk mitigation into steps deciding who is going to do what and by when.

6 Risk monitoring: deciding on the governance process for how management will monitor risk management plans to ensure follow-through using regular risk meetings, putting risk as an agenda item in project meetings, virtual meetings and so on.

It all sounds very logical so why doesn't it work particularly well in practice?

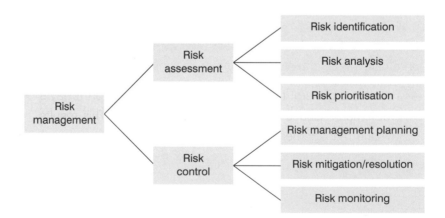

Problems with traditional risk management

The most fundamental problem comes down to the psychology of risk and language. With business, and projects in particular, it is all about achieving objectives by set timescales, i.e. positive activities. Risk is a **negative** concept so to get people to think and talk openly about their risks can be quite a challenge. For example, when you ask a project manager, 'What are your risks?' this can have two main effects:

1 The project manager's brain is naturally thinking positively (i.e. 'What do I need to do?') and is suddenly asked a question that is pushing in completely the opposite direction (i.e. 'What could go wrong?'). The effect is to 'confuse' the brain so that it starts thinking about things that might go wrong but are not necessarily linked to the objectives of the project. This generates spurious risks such as the building falling down or flooding. These may be 'risks' but they are very low probability (hopefully) and should not be the concern of, or managed by, the project manager in any case.

2 The project manager immediately starts to think things like 'What are you going to do with this information?' and may feel threatened if you share their fears with colleagues and superiors. The effect will be to tell you what risks they are actually comfortable about managing and not the ones that are their real concerns.

This psychological barrier can significantly compromise risk identification and therefore can subsequently undermine the whole risk management process.

In addition there are further problems with traditional approaches that compromise quality and efficiency:

→ There is a general tendency for people to focus on today's problems or 'issues' rather than tomorrow's risks. This results in issue management (reactive) rather than risk management (proactive). You need to implement risk management (fire prevention) or you will always be managing issues (fire fighting).

→ Risk statements (e.g. 'insufficient resources') are captured which are too generic to communicate the real concerns and therefore cause unnecessary confusion and give no insight to guide risk planning. This furthers the perception that the risk process is not adding value. At the opposite end of the scale, some risk statements may resemble essays and therefore never get read by busy managers.

→ Quantitative analysis is often based on wild numerical guesses and leads to incorrect prioritisation and inappropriate action. People tend to concentrate on the risks that they can quantify, for example contractual penalties or direct cost of resources, and play down risks that have 'softer' impacts that can't be quantified, such as impacts on quality, relationships or reputation.

→ Qualitative analysis is often based on HML type scales that leads to a default rating as medium risk exposure and inappropriate prioritisation so that it is impossible to 'see the wood for the trees'; for example, High Impact × Low Probability = Medium Risk Exposure.

→ Such risk analysis results in very little real action other than work that was already planned and therefore the team does not see any significant value in the risk management process. The actions required to manage the risks are not specific and therefore not followed through.

Traditional risk management approaches can be made to work by competent leaders and good teams but the administrative overhead involved in managing the problems described above tends to mean that, at best, the benefits are not justified by the cost and effort required to implement and support the risk management process.

Assumptions not risks

The key challenge with traditional risk management is the negativity aspect. So if we approach risk management from a positive perspective we avoid this problem. But risks are negative so how can you be positive about a negative concept?

Identification of risks is the wrong place to start – where do risks originate? Risks do not exist in isolation. The risk is always to 'something' and that something is a set of objectives. For any business venture, we have to identify our objectives, i.e. what we are trying to achieve. We can then define the risks relative to the objectives. The problem with this is that objectives are, by their very nature, high level and concise and therefore the risks will also be defined at a very high level. We have to take this a stage further.

If the objectives define what we are trying to achieve, then the plans describe how we are going to achieve them. So we define the risks relative to the plans – correct? Well, nearly.

Plans consist of some facts and a lot of assumptions. If the plan is to be successful, then the assumptions will turn into facts. Some assumptions will be close to being facts and we should not concern ourselves with them. Inevitably, many assumptions will be at risk and these are where we need to focus, i.e. on assumptions, not risks.

Communication and risk

The other side of the problem of ineffective risk management is communication – or lack of it. The root cause of all risk is communication – or lack of it. This is a bold statement but if we exclude 'acts of God' every risk could be avoided by early and appropriate communication. Let's look at some examples:

→ A project is planning to undertake system testing in May. In the last week of April the team discover that another project is dominating the test facility and will continue to do so until the end of June. This leads to a minimum delay of one month. If the test facility schedule had been communicated to the appropriate people early enough, alternative arrangements might have been possible.

→ A production line breaks down, leading to three days of no products being output. It emerges that the component that failed had shown signs of fatigue for several months. If the people who knew this had communicated it to the production manager, preventative maintenance at the weekend might possibly have prevented the major failure.

→ A company has invested heavily in a new product that will provide additional functionality to their most important client. After six months of development they demonstrate the new product only to find out that their client's strategy is changing and the functionality will be wasted. If the account manager had communicated their intentions to their client six months earlier, they would have realised that this initiative was not a good idea.

So it should be clear that risk can be avoided by appropriate communication at the appropriate time. But what should be communicated? In a world of information overload it will be too easy to communicate so much that it will be ignored; if we communicate too little, risks will sneak through the cracks. We need to communicate 'just enough' and that criterion is met by the assumptions that we make. Our assumptions will cover the resources we need, the timescales we plan, the interdependencies we see, the complexities we understand, the decisions we are relying on and so on.

For example, if we wanted to communicate everything we need people to know about our project, we might consider distributing a detailed project plan. But very few people would even look at it. At the other end of the scale we might consider communicating the objectives and a couple of key milestones in an email. People might read that but it will not help avoid the majority of potential risks. However, if we capture the key assumptions that we are making, say 20 of them, and cross-communicate these to the key stakeholders, we are communicating something which is valuable and will probably be read.

ABCD risk management – a better way?

ABCD stands for 'Assumption Based Communication Dynamics' as it uses the cross-communication of assumptions as its core principle. ABCD was developed in the early 1990s to address the fundamental problems encountered with traditional risk management processes, as summarised above. It has evolved and been used successfully in hundreds of enterprises around the world. However, the core principles are just the same as those originally developed. Many of the principles of ABCD have been adopted over the years into traditional approaches but, as an integrated process, ABCD is still probably the most effective and efficient risk management process around, based on the author's experience.

That said, this is not a book about implementing a fully integrated ABCD process. This is a book about the principles of ABCD. What I have tried to do is to take the fully integrated ABCD process and extract the valuable nuggets to allow you to apply some or all of its principles as you choose.

If you have an existing risk management process that you are committed to using, you can integrate the principles that work for you. If you are starting up a new risk management process from scratch, you can implement all the principles for an integrated ABCD approach.

So what about issues?

Risks are significant uncertainties that might happen in the future. Issues are significant events that have already happened.

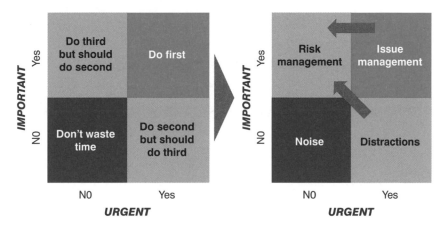

Risk and issue management tends to get wrapped up in the same package, which is theoretically fine but practically problematic. To explain the problem, look at Stephen Covey's principles for time management as described in his book, *The 7 Habits of Highly Effective People*.[1] Covey says that everything we do in life is either urgent or important and we prioritise subconsciously around these parameters. We will obviously do the important/urgent stuff first but then tend to get dragged into the not important/urgent tasks just because they are 'urgent'. As Covey explains, we have to do some important/not urgent tasks in order to avoid being stuck in the important/urgent sector. See the figures above.

[1] Covey, S. (2004) *The 7 Habits of Highly Effective People*, Simon & Schuster Ltd.

And so it is with business. The important/urgent are issues – they have already happened so they need to be dealt with. Having dealt with them we must not be distracted into the not important/urgent stuff. Use this time to deal with the important/not urgent i.e. the risks. Risks are clearly important – if they are not managed, they will become issues. But they should not be urgent by their very nature as they should be dealt with as they emerge over the horizon.

QUICK TIP ISSUE MANAGEMENT VS RISK MANAGEMENT
Spend at least some time on risk management or you will always be stuck in issue management.

Issues come in all shapes and sizes but generally:

→ Small issues will be fixed there and then and there is no requirement for a formal process to control them.

→ Big issues will require plans to fix them. The plans will have assumptions and it's the assumptions that we should assess for risk. Track the assumptions in the plans to fix the issues, not the issues themselves.

→ Following this logic, we should not have many or even any significant issues at any point in a venture as we should be focusing on assumptions. These are Covey's observations transported into a risk management context.

For the occasional 'big' issue, formal issue management should be a relatively simple process. Issues should be prioritised for:

→ Size – how big are the issues relative to each other? A simple red, amber, green scale will suffice.

→ Controllability – how easy will the issue be to solve?

→ Urgency – how soon does the issue (really) need to be solved?

Rank your issues based on these ratings and then get on with setting actions and fixing them. We will not be looking at issues again in this book.

QUICK TIP ISSUES VS ASSUMPTIONS

Don't focus on the issue; focus on the assumptions within the plans to fix the issue and manage the risks to these assumptions.

When risk management fails

If risk management were as simple as described in this chapter, we would not need the rest of this book. Sadly, as is common with most things in life, it's a bit more complicated than that. The common reasons for risk management failing are:

→ Important risks are not identified.

→ Risk are identified but not prioritised correctly.

→ Risks are identified but not mitigated or inappropriate actions taken.

A perfect example of this is the recent financial crisis. Banks went bust because they:

→ failed to identify fundamental risks, and/or

→ focused on specific risks without considering the compound effects of risks, and/or

→ consciously or subconsciously decided to ignore the risks and their analyses.

This was exacerbated by the focus on 'traditional' financial risk management at the expense of 'operational' risk management. This meant that operational risks were not prioritised correctly and ultimately little or no action was taken. Specifically 'experts' made assumptions about the upward trend of the housing market that proved to be untrue and the value of banks' assets was eventually undermined.

You will, I hope, be operating in a slightly less risky environment but you will need to look out for exactly the same problems and behaviours. The key is to get the right balance between simplicity and complexity to achieve effective risk management and to provide demonstrable value. The audit view of risk management is valuable in its context, but just ticking boxes will only avoid problems in the simplest of ventures. As soon as things get big and complex, you need robust processes and tools to navigate your way to success. This book will help you to achieve this.

Everything should be made as simple as possible, but not one bit simpler. Albert Einstein

So just what is risk management? – frequently asked questions

The following table provides quick answers to some of the most frequently asked questions about the topic of risk management, as summarised in Chapter 1. Use this as a way of gaining a quick overview.

FAQ 1 What is enterprise risk management (ERM)?	1 ERM is a process by which the total risk to the business is identified, prioritised and managed appropriately. In recent times, ERM has become a Holy Grail for organisations, i.e. if you can properly manage the total risk to the business, then you should be able to sleep at night. In reality full ERM is often a valiant aim rather than an achievable reality for most businesses, and setting risk strategy is more about scoping what is possible now and what is desirable in the future.
FAQ 2 Where does financial risk management fit into ERM?	2 Financial risk management (e.g. credit risk, market risk etc.) is a sub-set of ERM. Very often the sum of all the financial risk management tools is called ERM but this does not include operational risks, programme/project risks or strategic risks which can be just as important as pure financial risk, if not more so.
FAQ 3 What is strategic risk management?	3 Strategic risk management assesses and manages the risk to your business objectives/strategy. This requires a top-down view of risk that looks at both internal and external constraints and also should include escalated risks from projects and operations that may have an impact on the strategy.
FAQ 4 What is the difference between risk management and issue management?	4 Issues are problems that have already occurred. Risks are potential problems that have a potential to occur but may not. Issue management is important but is effectively 'fire fighting'. Issue management is minimised by effective risk management.

FAQ 5 What is ABCD risk management?	5 ABCD is 'Assumptions Based Communication Dynamics', a process that was specifically developed to mitigate the practical failings in traditional risk management processes. ABCD has a portfolio of techniques including Quality Based Costing and Quick Assumption Check but the core process is Assumption Analysis.
FAQ 6 How does assumption analysis work?	6 Assumption analysis is a technique that allows risks to be identified, analysed and managed from a positive perspective, i.e. rather than asking 'What are your risks?' you can ask 'What are the things that need to happen in order for you to be successful, i.e. your assumptions?' Analysis of the assumptions reveals the assumptions that are at risk. All risks have underlying assumptions.
FAQ 7 How do we prioritise risks?	7 Risks should be prioritised against the overall objectives (i.e. strategy, programme, project or operations). The key measures are criticality (i.e. the overall impact), controllability (i.e. the confidence that you can mitigate) and urgency (i.e. how soon you need to act). Graphical representations such as bubble diagrams will help you to see priorities clearly.
FAQ 8 Why do we need to prioritise projects/ operations?	8 For strategic or programme risk assessments, the first stage is to prioritise the projects and/or operations. This will ensure that resources are focused appropriately and projects/operations only raise risks to an appropriate level (e.g. minor projects should not be able to flag critical risks to the programme). The key measures for project/process prioritisation are business criticality (i.e. assessing by how much the business will be impacted if the project/operations fail) and complexity (i.e. how (relatively) complex the project/operational process is).
FAQ 9 What is risk governance?	9 Risk governance is the process by which risk management is made to work in a practical sense. It includes the use of effective risk registers, risk review boards (RRBs) and the procedures (rules) that define how the risk process will operate.
FAQ 10 How do you keep risk plans effective and efficient?	10 Risk plans tend to be unstructured and ineffective if not set up and managed rigorously. They can easily be too high-level and generic and therefore lead to inactivity. By focusing on managing the specific underlying assumption(s) the plans can be focused and easily actionable.
FAQ 11 How do risk management roles and responsibilities work?	11 The traditional risk management role of one risk owner for each risk tends to lead to inaction and blame. Having a senior risk owner and a separate risk action manager for each risk provides the checks and balances that ensure follow-through of risk actions.

FAQ 12 How do you set up a risk review board (RRB)?	**12** The traditional risk meeting can tend to be a 'talking shop' where considerable time is spent discussing very few risks. The RRB is designed to ensure that the right people are focused on to the root causes of risks and therefore spend the minimum effective time clarifying risks, prioritising and agreeing risk plans. All senior risk owners should attend the RRB.
FAQ 13 How can we measure risk management effectiveness?	**13** The prioritised risks should be managed in priority order to have the greatest impact on the overall risk profile. This is often best done using a visual representation like the bubble diagrams where the trend shown by taking a snapshot of the bubble diagram each month (for instance) will quickly show if the risk profile is improving or deteriorating. More detailed techniques such as analysing the underlying risk drivers may also be useful.
FAQ 14 What is the difference between a risk manager and a risk administrator?	**14** The term 'risk manager' has become misinterpreted in many businesses. In most respects, the risk manager is not in a position to manage the risks, i.e. they do not have the insight or the resources and their role should be focused on the risk process. Hence the term risk administrator is more appropriate.
FAQ 15 How do we minimise risk administration?	**15** Administration is a necessary evil for all forms of management but it has to be kept to a reasonable level or the perception may be that the effort is not matched by the benefits. Modern software tools will help to reduce the paperwork but the process needs to justify its existence by helping the team members to identify and manage risks in ways that they would not do intuitively (i.e. the need for demonstrable value).
FAQ 16 How can we motivate appropriate risk management behaviour?	**16** Basic metrics will show you how effective people are at following through and will help to motivate positive behaviour. Appropriate measures are time-open for each risk, average time-open for each risk owner, actions-open for each risk action manager, etc. Include risk management effectiveness as a formal criterion in performance evaluations.
FAQ 17 What is groupthink?	**17** When groups make decisions, they may well take more risks than the individuals themselves would – this is 'groupthink'. Groupthink tends to occur when a group strives to reach consensus despite the fundamental concerns of the individuals.
FAQ 18 How do you minimise groupthink?	**18** You could: • use external experts to challenge the group thinking • set up multiple groups working on the same issue • appoint a 'devil's advocate' for key meetings to test conclusions • ensure that senior management avoid expressing opinions before key meetings/projects.

FAQ 19 How do we take opportunities?	**19** Risk can have both an upside as well as a downside. We call this upside risk 'opportunity'. Most traditional risk management approaches struggle to identify opportunities because this requires a complete shift in thinking (i.e. thinking positively rather than negatively). ABCD makes this process easier as the assumptions are positive and can be assessed relative to what was planned, i.e. the outcome could be better as well as worse than assumed. Opportunities should be prioritised in a similar way to risks to make sure that the big opportunities are seized.
FAQ 20 How do you 'sell' risk management?	**20** Risk is generally considered to be a 'negative' subject and therefore it can be difficult to motivate people to give it appropriate attention. ABCD can help as it naturally provides a positive perspective via the assumption focus. Highlighting opportunities also helps as the upside is emphasised. Ultimately, though, you need to convince people that the use of formal risk management will identify at least one big risk that would have remained undetected and the process will therefore pay for itself many times over, making everyone's job easier.

We hope these FAQs give a quick start to getting to grips with Fast Track risk management. The rest of this book shows you how to move from understanding what the key elements of risk management are to an active implementation of a new risk management system or the improvements to an existing risk management system within your team, division or companywide.

Risk managers and the future
Professor Steve Tippins Roosevelt University, LA Crosse, Wisconsin, Canada

As little as three years ago it would have been easy to conclude that risk management as a profession had missed the boat and would be relegated to a support position down the organisational chain. Financial managers and their securitisation tools were in vogue and traditional risk management procedures and techniques did not provide the returns promised by securitisation, and risk managers in general did not have the financial expertise to head these new risk management activities. Securitisation in its many forms looked like it might relegate risk managers back to the role of insurance buyers.

The collapse/upheaval of the financial markets has been well chronicled. Its impact on risk management has received little attention. With recession and its impact on securitisation, risk managers and their tools are getting more attention. While this is good it is not the time for the risk management profession to say 'I told you so' and rest on their resurgence.

Risk managers got into the position they faced before the recession because few people in their organisations understood the breadth and scope of their activities or their value to the firm. If you prevent something from happening it is difficult to design a metric that shows management the value of a prevented loss. This has always been a problem for risk managers and was more so when financial managers showed techniques that securitised risk and posited positive returns.

Now is the time for the risk management profession to step into the void and add all the tools of risk management to their toolbox. Enterprise risk management (ERM) has been evolving for 20 years. Securitisation seemed to take over the term for a time but now risk managers have the chance to redefine ERM in a truly broad scope and, if done properly, include securitisation in their portfolio.

When it comes to the bottom line, investors do not care if money was made or lost from sales, a currency hedge or a fire. It has been said that good management is good risk management and this is true. Risk managers need to step up and fill the void left by the financial crisis and define the risk management landscape, including the appropriate tools for the appropriate situation.

At the same time, risk managers must look beyond this opportunity to the future. How will risk managers incorporate sustainability, full cost accounting, the triple bottom line, and other pressures facing business as it moves forward?

One of the most exciting things about the field of risk management is the opportunity to look at all phases of business and society. Risk management as a profession currently has a unique opportunity to craft its future and help all parties move into the future. If industry leaders can grab this opportunity they will put the profession in a position to grow and thrive.

RISK MANAGEMENT PROCESS AUDIT

In order to improve performance you first need to understand what your starting point is, what your strengths and weaknesses are and how each will promote or limit what you can achieve. There are two levels of awareness you need to have. The first is to understand what the most effective risk managing teams look like, how they behave and how near your team is to emulating them. The second is to understand what it takes to lead such a team – do you personally have the necessary attributes for success?

Team assessment

Is my team really capable of managing risk?

Use the following checklist to assess the current state of your team, considering each element in turn. Use a simple Red-Amber-Green evaluation, where Red reflects areas where you disagree strongly with the statement and there are significant issues requiring immediate attention, and Amber suggests areas of concern and risk. Green suggests that you are comfortable with the current situation.

ID	CATEGORY	EVALUATION CRITERIA	STATUS
R1	Leadership	Risk management is a strategic priority: it is owned by a member of the senior executive team, and its importance has been cascaded down through all management levels	
R2	Attitude	Senior management actively supports the creation of joint risk management processes with clients. Openness and collaboration are high priorities when discussing risk	
R3	Roles and responsibilities	Risk management is an integrated part of roles and responsibilities and is consistent across the enterprise	
R4	Process	Teams are fully trained in a common risk management process and are effective in its application	
R5	Escalation	Teams are fully aware of audit responsibilities and understand how and when to escalate risks	
R6	Projects and implementation	Risk management initiatives follow best practice project management principles, have sufficient resources and budget, and address issues and risks	
R7	Support systems	There is a common web-based tool that provides visibility and control over the business, ensures teams follow a common process, reduces administration and encourages continuous learning	
R8	Opportunity management	Teams think equally in terms of identifying and realising opportunities as they do risks	
R9	Risk culture	There is a culture of risk awareness, where management have embraced risk management and walk the talk	
R10	Performance management	You have agreed key performance indicators for your risk management framework, a clear process for review and a culture of learning and improvement	

Tip

QUICK TIP BE PREPARED TO LEARN
No matter how good you think that you are at risk management, there are always better ways.

Having identified where the gaps are in your business or team capabilities, you need to understand if you are the right person to be leading the team as a leader in risk management.

Self-assessment

Do I have what it takes?

This section presents a self-assessment checklist of the factors that make a successful Fast Track leader in risk management. These reflect the knowledge, competencies, attitudes and behaviours required to get to the top, irrespective of your current level of seniority. Take control of your career, behave professionally, and reflect on your personal vision for the next five years. This creates a framework for action throughout the rest of the book.

Use this checklist to identify where you personally need to gain knowledge or skills. Fill it in honestly and then get someone who knows you well, your boss or a key member of your team, to go over it with you. Be willing to change your assessment if people give you insights into yourself that you had not taken into account.

Use the following scoring process:

0 *Not yet recognised as a required area of knowledge or skill*

1 *You are aware of the risk management area but have little knowledge and lack skills*

2 *It is an area where you are reasonably competent and working on improvement*

3 *It is an area where you have a satisfactory level of knowledge and skills*

4 *You are consistently well above average*

5 *You are recognised as a key figure in this area of knowledge and skills throughout the business.*

Then reflect on the lowest scores and identify those areas that are critical to success. Flag these as status 'Red' requiring immediate attention. Then identify those areas that you are concerned about and flag those as status 'Amber', implying areas of development that need to be monitored closely.

ID	CATEGORY	EVALUATION CRITERIA	SCORE	STATUS
	Knowledge		0–5	RAG
K1	Industry and markets	Knowledge of your industry sector in terms of scope (boundaries), overall size and growth, and major trends. This should include an understanding of the natural segmentation of products and markets		
K2	Customers and competitors	Information about major customers, in terms of who they are, and their must-haves and wants. Also an understanding of who the best competitors are and what they do, and supply chain options and capabilities		
K3	Products and services	An understanding of current products and services, and how they perform in the marketplace against the industry leaders. This should include substitutes or solutions available from companies in different industries		
K4	Business drivers	Insights into current and emerging technologies, legislation and environmental and economic trends that will impact on future product design, access to market or process improvements		
	Competencies			
C1	Project management	Understanding of basic project management tools and techniques. Ability to define, plan, monitor and control change activities in order to deliver identified performance improvements on time and within budget		
C2	Interpersonal skills	Ability to engage with superiors, peers and subordinates in a constructive way that will allow the risk process to flourish		
C3	Analytical thinking	Ability to think clearly about problems and follow processes rigorously		
C4	Risk management	Ability to think ahead and identify, prioritise and mitigate barriers to effective and enduring implementations of changes. Practise what you preach.		

ID	CATEGORY	EVALUATION CRITERIA	SCORE	STATUS
Attitudes			0–5	RAG
A1	Positive approach	Belief that you can make a difference and get things done. Avoidance of looking like a victim of circumstances when you have to overcome resistance from other people		
A2	Seeking synergies	Willingness to look for ways to creatively combine several ideas (even if they are other people's) in order to develop a new and exciting concept		
A3	Inquisitive mindset	Awareness of the need to constantly seek more effective or efficient ways of doing things. Willingness to challenge the status quo and ask why things are as they are		
A4	Breakthrough thinking	Not accepting average or second best. Constantly seeking ways to dramatically change the way things are		
Behaviours				
B1	Determination and commitment	Being prepared to see things through. No project goes exactly according to plan; you are not put off by early setbacks or problems – you need resilience		
B2	Visible and active support	Making it clear that you are supportive of priority ideas in the way you allocate your time, resources and budgets		
B3	Encouraging others	Enthusiastic in coaching and mentoring others who have ideas, or who are involved in the implementation of ideas. Looking for ways in which you can be the catalyst for the team		
B4	Positive challenge	Challenge the ideas of others in a positive way, helping them to think differently about the way things are		

QUICK TIP OPEN TO IDEAS
Ask members of your team how open they think you are to
new ideas.

Note that the importance of the evaluation criteria will change with your
exact role and business situation. Therefore you should use the rankings
to paint an appropriate picture of priorities. For instance, in many situations, a deep understanding of your business sector will be essential.
However, it is entirely possible to set up and perform risk management
without deep industry experience by following rigorous processes and
harnessing the knowledge of the business. In many ways this is the
most effective way of risk identification and analysis as you do not cloud
the results with your preconceptions.

Audit summary

Take a few minutes to reflect on the leadership–team effectiveness
matrix opposite and consider your current position: where are you and
what are the implications?

→ Bottom left – poor leadership and an ineffective team will result
   in failure. Who knows, you may already be too late.

→ Top left – great leadership but a poor team implies that you
   have a great vision but you will be unlikely to implement it and
   so it will have little impact. You will need to find a way of developing and motivating the team, and introducing systems and
   processes to improve team effectiveness.

→ Bottom right – poor leadership but a great team implies you
   are highly effective and efficient as a team but may well be
   going in the wrong direction.

→ Top right – clear leadership and direction combined with an
   efficient and effective team. This is where we want to be. An
   effective risk management focused team led by a visionary
   leader. You don't need this book; please give it to someone else!

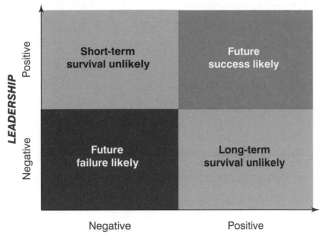

TEAM EFFECTIVENESS

STOP – THINK – ACT

At the end of the individual and team audits take time to reflect on your profile in order to do the following.

1 Identify any 'quick wins' you could change today.

2 See which chapters in this book could help the most.

Look for areas where you could get a 'quick win' and improve matters in the short term. Ask yourself and the team these questions:

What should we do?	What will you change today, and what difference will it make (why)? How will we know if it has been successful?
Who do we need to involve?	Who else needs to be involved to make it work and why?
What resources will we require?	What information, facilities, materials, equipment or budget will be required and are they available?
What is the timing?	When will this change be implemented – is there a deadline?

Visit **www.Fast-Track-Me.com** to use the Fast Track online planning tool.

The following expert stresses the importance of BS 31100. Standards are very important and BS31100 should raise the game for risk management across businesses. However, it only provides a risk management framework into which specific processes need to be applied. For instance, the standard may talk about risk identification options but does not mandate one type. In this context, assumption analysis can be used to identify risks effectively without being in conflict with the standard. I stress this point as the reader may misinterpret what follows as a 'push' for traditional risk management approaches that we have explained the weaknesses of – it is not.

Risk management standards and processes

Dr Steve Simister Henley Business School, University of Reading

Anyone involved in risk management needs to have a good understanding of the relevant codes and standards applicable to the area of activity. Whilst there is no one standard or code which is universally accepted, in the United Kingdom, in particular, BS31100 is widely used.

BS 31100[1] is a key standard for risk management. It gives you an understanding of how to develop, implement and maintain effective risk management within your business. Using BS 31100 effectively can help you increase your company's effectiveness.

Organisations of all types and sizes face a range of risks affecting the achievement of their objectives. While 'risk' is normally regarded as negative, risk management is as much about exploiting potential opportunities as preventing potential problems. It is important to bear this in mind whenever managing risk, and when reading this standard. Risk management is an essential part of good management.

Effective risk management helps you achieve your objectives by:

→ reducing the likelihood of events that would have a negative impact on your business

→ increasing the likelihood of events that would have a positive impact on your business

→ identifying opportunities where taking risks might benefit your business

[1] *BS 31100 – Risk management. Code of practice*, October 2008, http://shop.bsigroup.com/en/ProductDetail/?pid000000000030191339

→ improving accountability, decision making, transparency and visibility

→ identifying, understanding and managing multiple and cross-organisation risks

→ executing change more effectively and efficiently and improving project management

→ providing a better understanding of, and compliance with, relevant governance, legal and regulatory requirements, and corporate social responsibility and ethical requirements

→ protecting your revenue and enhancing value for money

→ protecting your reputation and stakeholder confidence

→ proactively managing your organisation's operations

→ controlling expenditure and delivering a cost-optimal control environment

→ retaining and developing customers by being more flexible and responsive to their needs.

The benefits of good risk management (and the consequences of poor risk management) will be felt by you, your staff, shareholders, customers and other stakeholders.

BS 31100 establishes the principles and terminology for risk management. It also gives recommendations for the model, framework, process and implementation of risk management gained from experience and good practice. It should be used for:

→ ensuring that your business achieves its objectives

→ ensuring risks are proactively managed in specific areas or activities

→ overseeing risk management in your company

→ providing assurance on your risk management strategy

→ reporting to stakeholders, e.g. through annual financial statements, corporate governance reports or corporate social responsibility reports.

This key standard for risk management is useful to CEOs, CFOs, CROs, CIOs, COOs and CTOs; chairmen and company secretaries; managing, IT and finance directors; risk, insurance, claims and business continuity managers; information security specialists; underwriters; health and safety officers; and heads of legal affairs.

For those involved in managing projects, BS6079 Part 3[2] presents guidance on the identification and control of business related risks encountered when undertaking projects. It is applicable to a wide spectrum of project organisations operating in the industrial, commercial and public or voluntary sectors. It is written for project sponsors and project managers, either or both of whom are almost always responsible to higher levels of authority for one or more projects of various types and sizes.

This standard offers generic guidance only and it is not suitable for certification or contractual purposes. It is not intended as a substitute for specific standards that address risk assessment in distinct applications, such as health and safety, or areas of technological risk. It is intended that its application will be proportional to the circumstances and needs of the particular organisation. The guidance in this standard highlights the importance of stakeholder analysis and suggests that it is integrated into the risk management process.

For those working in specific sectors such as defence procurement or insurance there are specific guidelines. These may vary from the British Standard, as might standards used in other parts of the world.

ISO 31000:2009[3] provides principles and generic guidelines on risk management. It can be used by any public, private or community enterprise, association, group or individual. Therefore, ISO 31000:2009 is not specific to any industry or sector. It can be applied throughout the life of an organisation, and to a wide range of activities, including strategies and decisions, operations, processes, functions, projects, products, services and assets. It can also be applied to any type of risk, whatever its nature, whether having positive or negative consequences.

Although ISO 31000:2009 provides generic guidelines, it is not intended to promote uniformity of risk management across organisations. The design and implementation of risk management plans and frameworks will need to take into account the varying needs of a specific organisation, its particular objectives, context, structure, operations, processes, functions, projects, products, services or assets and specific practices employed.

It is intended that ISO 31000:2009 be utilised to harmonise risk management processes in existing and future standards. It provides a common approach in support of standards dealing with specific risks and/ or sectors, and does not replace those standards. But it is not intended for the purpose of certification.

---

[2] *BS 6079 Part 3 – Project management. Guide to the management of business related project risk*, January 2000, http://shop.bsigroup.com/en/ProductDetail/?pid=000000000019994545
[3] *ISO 31000 – Risk management – Principles and guidelines*, http://webstore.ansi.org/RecordDetail.aspx?sku=ISO+31000%3a2009

PART B

BUSINESS FAST TRACK

I rrespective of your chosen function or discipline, look around at the successful managers whom you know and admire. We call these people Fast Track managers, people who have the knowledge and skills to perform well and fast track their careers. Notice how they excel at three things:

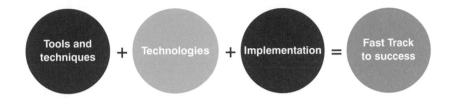

Tools and techniques

They have a good understanding of best practices for their particular field. This is in the form of methods and techniques that translate knowledge into decisions, insights and actions. They understand what the best companies do and have an ability to interpret what is relevant for their own businesses. The processes they use are generally simple to explain and form a logical step-by step approach to solving a problem or capturing data and insights. They also encourage creativity – Fast Track managers do not follow a process slavishly where they know they are filling in the boxes rather than looking for insights on how to improve performance. This combination of method and creativity produces the optimum solutions.

They also have a clear understanding of what is important to know and what is simply noise. They either know this information, or have it at their fingertips as and when they require it. They also have effective filtering mechanisms so that they don't get overloaded with extraneous information. The level of detail required varies dramatically from one situation to another – the small entrepreneur will work a lot more on the knowledge they have and in gaining facts from quick conversations with experts, whereas a large corporate may employ teams of analysts and research companies. Frequently when a team is going through any process, they uncover the need for further data.

Technologies

However, having the facts and understanding best practice will achieve little unless they are built into the systems that people use on a day-to-day basis. Fast Track managers are good at assessing the relevance of new information technologies and adopting the appropriate ones in order to maximise both effectiveness and efficiency.

Implementation

Finally, having designed the framework that is appropriate to them and their team, Fast Track managers have strong influencing skills and are also great at leading the implementation effort, putting in place the changes necessary to build and sustain the performance of the team.

How tightly or loosely you will use the various tools and techniques presented in Part B will vary, and will to a certain extent depend on personal style. As you read through the following three chapters, first seek to understand how each could impact you and your team, and then decide what level of change may be appropriate given your starting point, authority and career aspirations.

QUICK TIP *PEOPLE AND TOOLS*
Extraordinary people + average tools = average performance
but
Average people + extraordinary tools = extraordinary performance

FAST TRACK TOP TEN

This chapter presents a framework of methods or techniques to improve performance and make life as a risk manager easier. Each function can take a lifetime to master, but the Fast Track manager will know which areas to focus on – get those areas right and the team will perform. Often success relates to the introduction of simple tools and techniques to improve effectiveness and efficiency.

Introducing risk management tools and techniques

What needs to be included – the top ten tools and techniques

The 'top ten' tools and techniques are relevant to risk management professionals and to business/project managers generally:

1   **Enterprise risk management** – Starting with the big picture, how would you build a risk management framework to identify and manage the total risk to your business enterprise? Both quantitative and qualitative approaches are considered. All the remaining tools and techniques effectively fit into this framework.

2   **Strategic risk management** – It's no use managing the risk to your operations if your strategy is at risk so this should be your first point of focus.

3 **Assumption analysis** – Don't try to capture risks; analyse assumptions and approach risk management from a positive rather than a negative perspective.

4 **Prioritisation** – This is everything in any significant risk management process. If you fail to prioritise appropriately, you can't see the wood for the trees. Start by prioritising your projects and business processes and then prioritising your risks.

5 **Risk governance** – Explains how the risk process is applied to ensure effective and efficient follow-through on risk management. Includes the use of risk reporting, effective risk planning and risk escalation.

6 **Risk roles and responsibilities** – Defines the various risk related responsibilities that need to be implemented for effective risk management at the various levels in the organisation.

7 **Risk trends** – Measure the effectiveness of the risk process by analysing trends that will enable you to pinpoint and fix problems at a strategic rather than tactical level.

8 **Risk metrics and behaviour** – Set up metrics that will drive appropriate behaviours in the stakeholder group and improve risk management performance overall.

9 **Risk and groupthink** – How to identify and manage the particular risks associated with decision making in groups.

10 **Positive approaches to risk management** – How to turn a 'negative' subject into a positive experience by focusing on opportunities, learning how to 'sell' risk management and doing risk management jointly with clients and suppliers.

1 ENTERPRISE *Risk management*

In business, as in life, your starting point is always to establish your objectives or strategy. Set risk management strategy against an enterprise risk management (ERM) framework. ERM is a process by which the total risk to the business is identified, prioritised and managed appropriately. In recent times, ERM has become a Holy Grail for organisations, i.e. if you can properly manage the total risk to the business then you should be able to sleep at night. In reality full ERM is often a valiant aim rather than an achievable reality for most businesses, and setting risk strategy is more about scoping what is possible now and what is desirable in the future.

Define the 'enterprise' in terms of your world. For example, perhaps the enterprise is the business area that you are responsible for or even just the one project that you own. However, it is always best to 'shoot for the stars if you want to hit the moon' so let's consider how full ERM can be established in a business before defining and prioritising the various components.

The benefits of applying enterprise risk management

The key benefits that should be realised from applying effective ERM are improving both short-term and long-term business profitability and performance by:

→ avoiding costly mistakes – by capturing and managing risks to key projects and operational processes

→ validating strategy – by checking that all key stakeholders are 'on the same page' with strategic priorities

→ improving operational effectiveness – through the adoption of a systematic and structured approach

→ building relationships – by increasing the confidence of stakeholders/clients

→ preserving reputation – by avoiding corporate disasters and associated publicity

→ anticipating market trends – by ensuring that key market assumptions remain valid.

In all cases the benefits in ERM will massively outweigh the investment.

What are the challenges?

Full ERM is a very difficult state to attain. Why is this?

→ **Quantification is difficult or even impossible**. Some risks (e.g. financial, contractual) are easy to quantify whilst others are virtually impossible (e.g. quality, reputation, performance). Therefore when organisations attempt to quantify the total risk to the business they tend to mix 'good quality' data with 'poor quality' data and thus dilute the real value of the final result.

→ **Objectives are not consistent across the enterprise**. This leads to perceptions of risk that vary massively in different areas of the organisation. One area of the business may consider a particular risk to be 'minor' whilst another area considers the same risk to be a 'showstopper': for example, operations may think that a change programme delay is a minor problem whereas the board may consider that any delay is a disaster.

→ **Risk processes are not consistent across teams**. This leads to differing focus, analysis, prioritisation and management approaches. Again this makes it impossible to build a consistent picture of risks across the enterprise.

→ **Risk tools are not supported by effective process**. Very often, the use of software tools is the first attempt by an organisation to provide some consistency of risk management. However, if the tools are not backed up by an effective risk process, the effect can be one of GIGO (garbage in, garbage out) as poor quality data is captured, analysed and then presented as a 'high quality' result.

The most common mistake, particularly to be found in financial institutions, is to integrate the various financial risk management measures (e.g. credit risk or market risk) and to call this 'ERM'. Thus the organisation thinks that they are tracking 'total' risk when they are actually only looking at the bit that they find easy to measure. Consequently if, for example, a large change programme goes wrong, it happens off their ERM radar and can have a massive impact on the business.

At the highest level many businesses fail to define and scope their ERM strategy. This is not to say that they fail to build a complete ERM system, more that they fail to agree what they are trying to measure and don't recognise the difficulties they will face in building an effective ERM process. It is almost impossible to build a full ERM system from scratch. It is much better to prioritise which area of your business will benefit from improved risk management first and concentrate on that, adding the other components later as part of the overall ERM framework.

Quantified ERM

It will never be possible to achieve high-quality quantification across all types of business risk. However, where it is necessary to calculate total risk exposure, a simple model that will allow quantified risks to be combined is shown in the Total RM framework below.

The four components of this model are:

1 **Financial risk management**: this covers the traditional financial risk management processes that are in place in many businesses and all financial institutions and includes (but may not

be limited to) credit and market risk management. These tools and techniques are well established and consequently the risks are relatively easy to quantify.

2 **Strategic risk management**: this looks at the strategic market trends and tries to predict the risks that you might face in future. By their very nature, these risks will probably be very difficult to accurately quantify.

3 **Operational risk management**: this looks at the risks to your day-to-day business processes. Operations are ongoing by their nature in the business and therefore the risks should be relatively easy to quantify.

4 **Programme risk management**: these are the risks to your change programmes and projects. Their nature is such that accurate quantification will be difficult: for example, the knock-on effect from a specific risk in a project could have a massive financial impact downstream but this is going to be very difficult to establish.

(Tip) **QUICK TIP *TO QUANTIFY OR NOT TO QUANTIFY?***
You don't need to quantify risk in order to manage it. What is important is to be able to measure risks in some way to ensure that you can compare 'apples with apples' and therefore prioritise consistently across the enterprise, deciding which risks to resource and manage first. You can do this qualitatively, with the right approach.

Qualitative ERM

If we relax requirements to quantify every risk, you will find that it is much easier to compare, aggregate and prioritise risks across the enterprise. A tried and tested model for identifying, analysing, prioritising and combining enterprise risks is shown opposite.

This is a practical implementation of the total risk management framework with the financial risk management element removed. This is not to suggest that financial risk should be ignored – far from it – but it is meant to imply that you should continue to identify, quantify and manage financial risks using established processes and tools. If financial risk management is already in place in your organisation, don't waste time and energy by trying to make changes to the process. Simply take the quantitative output from financial risk management and convert it into a qualitative rating using an appropriate scale, for example:

Red = impact greater than €3m

Amber = impact between €1m and €3m

Green = impact less than €1m

Risks from the other components of the model should be evaluated qualitatively and only quantified on an exception basis, i.e. where this can be justified by the quality of the available data and where there is a clear need to have a quantified result.

The components of the Qualitative ERM model are as follows.

Strategic risk management
There is no point delivering products and projects on time and within budget if the market no longer wants them. Thus it is imperative to identify strategic assumptions and risks as the highest priority. Strategic risks will by definition have massive potential impacts. Techniques for effectively identifying strategic risks are included in the next top ten tip.

Operational risk management

These are the risks to the ongoing processes in the business (e.g. the risk that a production line will stop). Often operational risks are relatively easy to identify, as the processes are well established and staffed by experienced personnel. Operational risks are characterised by the predicted frequency of occurrence (e.g. how many times per year a component is likely to fail) based on historical data. Many organisations include their projects under 'operational risk' but this is often not a good idea as project risks do not have this historical data due to the 'one-off' nature of projects and tend to get lost in the mix with process-based risks when they deserve more attention. Operational risks which have a potential impact on the strategy are escalated to the strategic level.

Programme/project risk management

These are the risks that a project will fail to deliver (e.g. a new product/ overbudget/late etc.). Project risks are generally more difficult to identify than operational risks as projects are, by definition, trying to introduce something new to the organisation and therefore historical data does not exist. Risks within major change programmes are the most difficult of all to identify/prioritise/manage due to the programme complexity making it difficult to 'see the wood for the trees'. The impact of these risks is often massive if they relate to a critical change programme: for example, where delayed benefits could be unacceptable, or a merger integration programme where the impact on the share price could be dramatic if delivery is delayed. Programme and project risks that have a potential impact on the strategy are escalated to the strategic level.

Transformation risk management

Projects and programmes that result in significant change (such as new product development, mergers and acquisitions) will 'transform' the current business. This is often when the business is exposed to most risk as the pressures increase the risk to both the current operations (that have to accept the changes while continuing to run the business) and the projects trying to transform them (that get push-back from operations at crucial phases like testing). From a process perspective, transformation risk is often treated as part of programme or project risk management as the risks are more project based than process based.

Contingency planning

Strictly speaking, this is not 'risk management': risk management is about stopping risks occurring (i.e. is proactive) whereas contingency planning relates to what to do if the risk impacts (i.e. is reactive). However, this is an essential part of any ERM system where business continuity is paramount.

Where should we start to implement ERM?

To some extent, the answer depends on what your business priorities are and what risk processes you already have in place. However, if you are starting with a blank sheet of paper, establish a strategic risk management process first. The immediate impact of identifying strategic risks to the business cannot be overestimated. The next step will depend on how many projects the business undertakes: if they are numerous and/ or business critical then address this area next. Operations can take care of themselves to a great extent as their ongoing nature means that new risks will be rare – until a change comes along from a project (i.e. transformation). Ultimately, formalising the operational risk management space will be beneficial but it is probably the least urgent task in most businesses.

Prioritising risks across the enterprise

The starting point is to create a clear strategy statement for your business that encompasses all key operational and project objectives (i.e. capture key programme deliverables, milestone dates and operational process service level agreements and include 'softer' objectives like reputation building etc.). Do this as the first step in establishing a strategic risk management process. Once captured you can set up risk prioritisation ratings based on the strategic objectives.

Red =

→ 'showstopper', i.e. critical programme or process objective not met (e.g. milestone, service level agreement or reputational)

→ unacceptable cost impact to business

→ no possible or acceptable contingency plan.

Amber =

→ significant objective not met

→ delay of non-critical (but significant) project

→ unable to meet non-critical (but significant) service level agreement

→ significant cost impact to business

→ difficult contingency plan.

Green =

→ minor or localised objective not met

→ minor cost impact to business

→ contingency plan identified and acceptable.

These ratings will work in this form for most businesses but you should feel free to expand or amend them any way that makes them more relevant to your business. When the ratings are fleshed out you should have a reasonably rigorous rating system that will allow consistent prioritisation of risks from any area of the organisation. There should then be no arguments over which risks to deal with first and which can wait.

In summary, the key to successful ERM is to clearly define the scope of your 'enterprise' and be prepared to accept that you will not be able to quantitatively measure all aspects of business risk accurately; recognise and discriminate between good quality estimates and guesswork. Then set up a consistent qualitative rating system so that you can compare 'apples with apples' and therefore prioritise risks consistently across the organisation.

| | CASE STORY **PHARMACEUTICAL CHANGE PROGRAMME, SIMON'S STORY** |

Narrator Simon was promoted to be programme manager for a major change programme just as the Year 2000 crisis was starting to loom.

Context In business, priorities are often in conflict but never more so than when you are competing with a once in a lifetime potential crisis.

Issue Buy-in from stakeholders had been average to poor but since planning for the Year 2000 changes had started, things had gone from bad to worse.

Solution The strategic assumptions for the organisation were captured and evaluated by the major stakeholders to the change programme. The results showed that there was little consensus on priorities and highlighted why Simon was struggling to get resources, to get people to attend meetings and to achieve sign-offs. Simon managed to rerun the exercise by getting the same assumptions rerated by the same people but now assuming (hypothetically) that the Y2000 programme was not happening.

Learning The new results showed much more consensus and, therefore, as Y2000 was not going to wait, the strategic decision was taken to suspend the change programme for six months until the Y2000 programme had been completed. This ultimately proved very successful and showed how important appropriate prioritisation is in reducing risk, particularly at a strategic level.

2 STRATEGIC Risk management

Strategic risks are, by definition, the risks of you not achieving your business strategy. Therefore if you fail to identify and deal with your strategic risks you will fail as a business if the risks materialise. It's all pretty sobering stuff but few businesses take the time to assess their exposure to strategic risk appropriately. This is even more surprising when you consider that the effort involved in doing a strategic risk assessment is relatively small whilst the payback can obviously be huge.

Successful projects do not ensure success

Most businesses see risk management as a finance function. Sometimes formal risk processes are applied to significant projects or even critical business processes. This is all commendable but a project to deliver a new product to the marketplace may be delivered on time and to budget, yet will be deemed a failure if the market has changed while you were designing and manufacturing, and now no longer wants the product. This is a classic case of the business strategy failing due to unidentified risks materialising and, if the new product is a major part of your business strategy, could spell disaster.

Brainstorming threats is not the answer

Organisations that do try and consider strategic risk very often fall into the trap of just 'brainstorming' the potential threats. This can be a quick and relatively painless exercise but it very rarely identifies the real strategic risks to a specific business. This is because the exercise will probably look at generic threats and not consider what is truly going on in the business or the marketplace. Alternatively, consideration may be given to many factors that would be highly unlikely to impact your specific business and so introduces too many red herrings. In addition, if stakeholders do not buy into the threats, they will be very unlikely to play their role in taking action to manage or negotiate around the risks.

Assumptions analysis – not risk analysis – is the answer

An effective process to undertake a strategic risk assessment is to start, not too surprisingly, by making sure that you have captured a suitable statement of your business strategy. This should be done by the board of directors and needs to be as specific as possible, quantified and with target dates for achieving objectives.

Next, communicate this strategy statement to at least the next two levels down in the organisation, or even the whole organisation if the company is still relatively small. The aim at this stage is just to get general consensus, so set short timescales for feedback and take on board any relevant points.

The directors should then break down the strategy statement into its constituent assumptions, i.e. the things that need to happen to ensure that the strategy is achieved. Aim for about 10–20 assumptions and ensure that you consider both internal and external factors as much as possible.

Focusing on assumptions rather than risks is key as it allows people to think positively rather than negatively. Most people tend to feel more comfortable and open about discussing assumptions rather than risks. Assumption analysis is a core technique within the ABCD risk management process that I will expand on in later top ten topics.

QUICK TIP STRATEGY FIRST
Successful projects do not necessarily make a successful business – if the market or the competition has moved in the meantime you may be delivering something that is no longer required.

Testing strategic assumptions

Show the assumptions to the top-level management with whom you shared the original strategy statement, but this time get them to rate the assumptions so that you can understand exactly how they individually feel about them. The assumptions are analysed for risk using sensitivity (How sensitive are you if this assumption changes or goes wrong?) and stability (How stable/confident are you about this assumption?). The ABCD scales for sensitivity and stability are more about decision making than severity. The four-point scale is crucial so that there is deliberately no 'medium' and the transition between B and C in each case leads you to either take action or not.

For each assumption produce a sensitivity/stability 'scatter' diagram, as shown overleaf. Look for three different types of patterns. In the diagrams below each ellipse represents an individual's perspective and different colours could be used to indicate different organisational groups and so on.

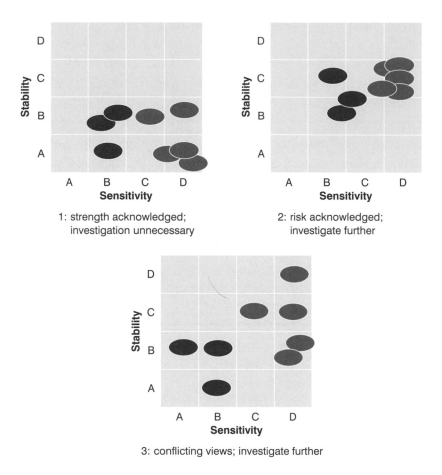

1: strength acknowledged;
investigation unnecessary

2: risk acknowledged;
investigate further

3: conflicting views; investigate further

Interpreting the results and taking action

In the first case the assumption is generally considered as likely to happen and therefore this can be considered as a strength of the strategy. If all your assumptions are rated in this way, you should revisit your strategy – it's not aggressive enough.

In the second case there is consensus that the assumption is at risk and the reasons behind this risk will require further investigation. If all your assumptions are rated in this way, your strategy is too aggressive and pursuing it is likely to result in failure and demoralisation.

In the third case there is little consensus and this could indicate a number of factors:

→ some people think that the assumption is at risk

→ others think that the assumption is a strength of the strategy

→ some people don't acknowledge that the assumption is important.

This is a very worrying result as it indicates that the organisation as a whole does not share a common view regarding the achievability of the strategy or even the importance of certain parts of the strategy. Also there is some risk here that could never have been identified by simple 'traditional' risk identification approaches, such as brainstorming.

For the second and third cases further investigation will be required to identify the root cause of the risks to the assumptions. The next stage will then involve the preparation of formal risk plans, in each case, to address the cause or remove the risk by trying to stabilise the underlying assumption or desensitise yourself to the effects of the assumption.

The importance of the external perspective

It should almost go without saying that the consideration of external factors is at least as important, if not more important, than internal factors. Whilst internal constraints like skills, available resources, etc. are important, they are things that will probably be considered implicitly in any case. However, external constraints will probably not be considered unless explicitly highlighted, for example:

→ market trends for the specific product or service being offered

→ competitors' likely strategy including pricing policy changes

→ socio-political shifts that may impact your business

→ macro- and microeconomic trends

→ global crises such as oil price rises or pandemics.

It is here where an external perspective can be extremely valuable. You might achieve this by the use of a non-executive director (or similar board representative) but the targeted use of a management consultant who specialises in your market could be the crucial difference between the analysis's success and failure and therefore between your business's success and failure. You will need external input from such people when formulating the assumptions and again when you want them to rate the assumptions to capture their perspective.

Once the analysis has been completed it should be revisited on a periodic basis (e.g. quarterly) as both the internal and external risks will change, both positively and negatively.

Options and scenarios

You may be faced with a situation that a number of fundamentally different scenarios could play out and each one could affect your strategy in a fundamentally different way. If this is the case, you may have to redo the analysis for different scenarios in order to be able to compare the risks emerging from each one. This is also a clear way of choosing between different strategic options based on the risks in each case. For example, you may have several different products that you are considering bringing to market. Instead of trying to assess the risk based on all the products, assess the risk to the strategy of bringing each product to market separately (and possibly in certain logical combinations).

Risk escalation

To complete the strategic risk picture, and to make it usable on an ongoing basis, include some mechanism for escalating risks from your key projects and your ongoing operational processes that may have strategic implications. Take care to keep this appropriate or the board may get swamped and lose perspective. Only the project/operational risks that have a potential impact on the business strategy, or risks that require board intervention, should be escalated. Identify and manage everything else at lower levels in the organisation.

Of course the other extreme here is that nothing gets escalated as teams are worried about the negative implications of revealing their risks. The answer is to use assumptions analysis in your projects and operations as well, but that's a subject for the next top ten topic.

Strategy is relative

As with enterprise risk management, your 'strategy' can be scoped in a similar way to your 'enterprise'. So, for example, the strategy of a significant project can be assessed using these techniques in just the same way as the strategy of the business is assessed.

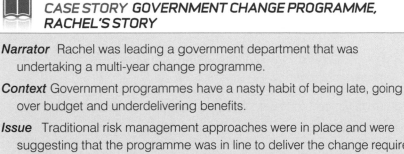

CASE STORY *GOVERNMENT CHANGE PROGRAMME, RACHEL'S STORY*

Narrator Rachel was leading a government department that was undertaking a multi-year change programme.

Context Government programmes have a nasty habit of being late, going over budget and underdelivering benefits.

Issue Traditional risk management approaches were in place and were suggesting that the programme was in line to deliver the change required in the department. Rachel was suspicious that all was not as well as it appeared.

Solution Rachel undertook an ABCD assumption-based strategic risk assessment that first captured the departmental strategy and cascaded this down to 12 key assumptions that would need to be met if the strategy was to be realised. These assumptions were then rated by the ten business area heads on an individual basis. Rachel then reviewed the results with all departmental heads together.

Learning There were major differences in opinion between business area heads that indicated that they were not in agreement on departmental strategy or on the programme being successful as planned. Rachel stopped the programme immediately and the new programme, re-scoped in line with the latest market requirements, was relaunched three months later and was ultimately successful.

3 ASSUMPTION *Analysis*

The assumption-based ABCD risk management process is a positive, rather than negative, way of identifying risks.

Assumption analysis works for both projects and ongoing business processes. However, as the former are generally more risky than the latter, we will focus on the project implementation of assumption analysis. Programme implementation requires prior prioritisation of the projects and subsequent prioritisation of their risks which are discussed in later top ten tips.

How the assumption analysis process works

Projects (and programmes) may apparently fail for lots of reasons but, at a fundamental level, there are basically three reasons:

1 The key assumptions we make are wrong.

2 We incorrectly assess the significance and/or confidence in these assumptions.

3 We fail to communicate the assumptions we make to all the key stakeholders.

Therefore assumptions are the source of all risks to the project/programme. The assumptions may be about resources, interdependencies, financing, timing, complexity, policy, etc. Therefore the capture, analysis, communication and management of the key assumptions being made in order to meet the programme/project objectives are key to successful risk management.

Clearly it is not possible to assess the risks that these assumptions pose to the programme or project unless the programme/project objectives are clear (i.e. without clear objectives, what is the risk to?). Therefore agree, document and communicate the programme and project objectives as a precurser to starting the assumption analysis process.

Capturing and analysing assumptions for risk

Having clarified the project objectives and produced at least high-level plans, identify the assumptions the team is making in order to achieve the objectives. Always capture a specific positive statement (e.g. 'the project will have 25 resources with business analysis skills by 1 March'), rather than the generic negative assessment that is traditionally captured (e.g. 'insufficient resources'). The idea is to focus on what needs to happen for the project to deliver to its objectives and to get people to think and communicate positively.

QUICK TIP ASSUMPTION ANALYSIS
All risks have underlying assumptions. Capture these and you will be closer to the root cause of the risk.

Assumptions should be specific and in the form of an explicit statement of '*something*…WILL happen…*in the future*'. Assumptions such as 'the project will have adequate resources…' are too generic and provide little insight to the reviewer so they need to be made more specific, for example 'ZZZ Testers will be available for the period y to z'.

Different techniques or prompts can be used to help to ensure that all key assumptions have been identified and analysed. The two primary techniques are structured interviews and workshops.

Structured interviews
Pros

→ Easier to capture specific and high-quality assumptions.

→ One-on-one encourages openness.

→ Tends to ensure complete/consistent analysis.

→ Takes less of the participants' time overall.

Cons

→ Needs dedicated risk management resources to undertake interviews.

→ Need to cross-communicate other assumptions that may be relevant as part of the interview.

Workshops
Pros

→ Gain instant consensus view on assumptions.

→ One session for risk identification.

→ Group dynamics can 'spark' new assumptions/risks.

Cons

→ Difficult to capture specific data.

→ Tends to take a long time to capture very little.

→ Can inhibit some participants who then do not contribute.

→ Takes significantly more of the participants' time overall.

QUICK TIP WORKSHOPS VS INTERVIEWS
On balance, interviews are more efficient than workshops at identifying risks.

In practice, a combination of interviews and workshops can work effectively (i.e. you can start the process off with interviews but when it's stable maintain it with workshops, returning to interviews at the start of a new stage). If in doubt, use interviews.

Look for different types of assumptions, i.e:

→ Explicit assumptions: get these directly from the plans (e.g. 'Unit testing will take no more than two weeks') and make sure that both internal assumptions and external assumptions (interdependencies) are captured.

→ Implicit assumptions: these cannot be captured by just analysing documentation but rely on interviewees' knowledge (e.g. 'Project XXX will have dedicated use of the testing facility during May' can only be evaluated if the interviewee has knowledge of what else is going on in the business around this time).

Make sure that all key assumptions are covered relating to milestones/timescales, resources, complexity and decisions.

Assessing assumptions for risk
The assumptions should then be assessed for risk. This is done, in the interview, by the assumption originator who rates the assumption in terms of two dimensions.

Sensitivity: How sensitive is the programme/project to assumption? How much does it matter if the assumption turns out to be wrong? In other words:

A = not sensitive/minor impact

B = manageable impact

C = significant Impact

D = very sensitive/critical impact.

Stability: How stable is the assumption? Are you very confident? In other words:

A = stable/very confident

B = fairly confident

C = uncomfortable

D = unstable/very uncomfortable.

Then plot assumptions on a matrix where the four squares at the top right, in particular, require close management attention as they represent assumptions that are both important and potentially unstable (see the figure overleaf). Treat assumptions in this quadrant as risky assumptions or 'risks'.

If different views are expressed about the sensitivity and stability, the worst case should always be accepted for the purposes of risk assessment. This forces communication between the 'optimists' and the 'pessimists' to resolve the disagreement and decide whether the concern is justified or not.

Finally capture the reasons for the sensitivity and stability ratings – this stage is crucial. The reason for the sensitivity ratings gives the (initial) impact if the assumption is a risk, and the reason for the stability rating pinpoints the concern and root cause of the risk. It is this latter concern that will often be the target of the mitigation plans if the assumption is at risk. Also the reasons for the sensitivity and stability will need to be communicated on the assumption/risk register so that other parties understand why the assumption is at risk and therefore what specifically needs to be done to bring it under control. For example:

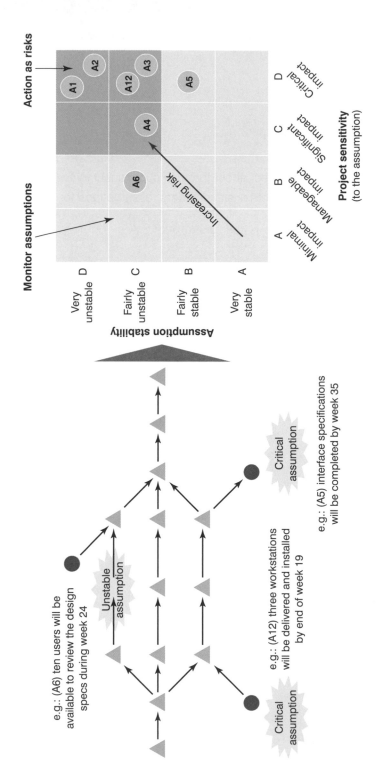

'Project XXX will have dedicated use of the testing facility during May'.

→ *Sensitivity = D. Why = testing is a critical path activity.*

→ *Stability = C. Why = project XYZ is entering testing around the same time period.*

The assumption register must be communicated widely to all key stakeholders in order that they see each other's assumptions and also understand how they feel about them. In subsequent interviews it may be appropriate to 'push' other stakeholders' assumptions for review by the interviewee. Remember, in any situation where someone 'disagrees' with an assumption's ratings, the most 'pessimistic view' always takes precedence.

QUICK TIP ASSUMPTION ANALYSIS
Cross-communication of assumptions identifies risks that traditional risk management processes could not have.

Assumption analysis process flow

The assumption analysis process can be summarised in a flow diagram, as below.

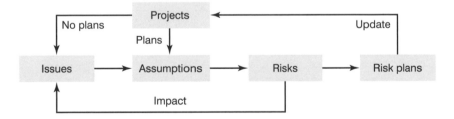

1 When a project is starting up, there are many issues that need to be resolved in order to formulate plans. If there are no formal plans, then there are no assumptions as such at this stage.

2 Plans consist of a few 'facts' and many assumptions so, as soon as basic plans are established, the key assumptions that they depend on need to be captured and analysed for risk.

3 Some assumptions are likely to happen or will not have a massive impact on the project if they don't. Some assumptions are more unstable and the project is very sensitive to them so they

may have a significant impact. These assumptions are treated as 'risks'.

4 Risks need to be managed so risk plans need to be set up to bring them under control.

5 Risk plans will update the project plans and, if the originator is confident that the revised plans will work, the risk may be closed. Alternatively the risk plan is monitored off-line from the project plans until the risk is considered to be resolved.

6 If a risk is not managed it will result in an issue. Small issues will be resolved quickly and do not need to be formally managed. Big issues will need plans to fix them. These plans will contain assumptions and these should be captured and processed as in steps 2–5 above.

QUICK TIP *ISSUES VS RISKS*

Issues are problems now. Risks are potential problems in the future. You have to focus on risks to avoid 'fire fighting' issues all the time.

 CASE STORY BANK MERGER INTEGRATION PROGRAMME, RICK'S STORY

Narrator Rick was responsible for, what was at the time, the largest ever bank merger integration programme.

Context The programme was tied to three key milestones which were immovable. Missing any one of these was likely to cause the share price to drop significantly and potentially destroy the business case for the bank merger.

Issue The bank's current risk management process was creaking under the strain with literally thousands of risks being raised in a haphazard way throughout the global business. Even worse was the number of issues being raised – and when analysed, many of the risks were in fact already issues.

Solution Rick commissioned an ABCD assumption-based process which was applied top-down to the programme. This very quickly identified the key assumptions that needed to be managed if the merger was to be successful and also removed the risk and issue 'noise' that was in the system, giving senior management clarity on where they needed to focus their attention.

Learning Rick learned to rely on the escalated risks rather than what his managers were telling him in progress meetings and this helped him to hit all three key milestones and achieve what the *Wall Street Journal* described as 'the textbook merger'.

4 PRIORITISATION *Risk and profits*

You need to prioritise risks so that you attack the right risks at the right time. In a multi-project environment or a programme you also need to prioritise the projects to make sure that you are focusing on the important and risky projects.

Risk prioritisation

If you are undertaking a relatively small project and therefore managing only a handful of assumptions/risks, the prioritisation in ABCD assumptions analysis (i.e. sensitivity and stability ratings) is enough to give you a prioritised register. However, as soon as projects get larger and more complex, you need a further level of prioritisation which should only be applied to the 'risky' assumptions (i.e. the risks).

The traditional way of prioritising risks is to use impact and probability. Multiply the two together to get a risk exposure and then rank your risks from highest to lowest risk exposure. This all sounds very logical but can be a distorted way of looking at risks:

→ Impact is often defined in terms of financial impact. This can cause problems as it is almost impossible to estimate the financial impact of risks that affect such things as quality, performance, reputation or relationships. In practice risks can have many types of impact and this is very difficult to represent in a simple rating or number.

→ Probability is very difficult for an individual to estimate. The definition of probability is 'how likely the risk is to occur if you take no action' and it is virtually impossible for you to think about a risk without also thinking about what you might do to manage it. Therefore you can't help factoring this into the estimate of probability, generally assessing it lower than it should be.

→ Time or urgency is not generally considered and this is a big mistake. For example, suppose you have a risk with a very big risk exposure that you can't do anything about for a year, and also a risk with a moderate risk exposure which is about to impact. Traditional approaches would suggest that you deal with the big risk first even though you might let the moderate risk impact while you are doing this.

Define a risk prioritisation system based on criticality, controllability and urgency.

Criticality This is effectively a multidimensional impact scale that can be tailored to suit your project or enterprise. A generic starting point for a project would be:

Red =

→ 'showstopper', i.e. critical project objective not met (e.g. deliverable, milestone, budget, reputational)

→ unacceptable cost impact to business

→ no possible or acceptable contingency plan.

Amber =

→ **significant** objective not met

→ significant cost impact to business

→ difficult contingency plan.

Green =

→ **minor** or localised objective not met

→ minor cost impact to business

→ contingency plan identified and acceptable.

Red is reserved for risks that will truly stop the project, as it is currently scoped, if they impact. Customise these ratings so that they clearly explain the risk to the documented project objectives. For operational processes the ratings are similar but will relate to production volumes, SLAs, metrics, etc.

Controllability This is a rating of how confident you are of bringing the risk under effective control. Controllability allows you to factor in 'what you could do to manage the risk' into your ratings (particularly after escalation) – in any case you will not be able to avoid thinking in this way:

→ **A = Very confident** that risk is controllable – e.g. risk plans established and high confidence that they will work.

→ **B = Fairly confident** that risk is controllable – e.g. outline risk plans in place and confident that they will work.

→ **C = Uncomfortable** that risk is controllable – e.g. no or few plans or low confidence that plans will work.

→ **D = Very uncomfortable** that risk is controllable – e.g. no plans and very low confidence that any effective plans can be established.

Controllability should not be confused with stability which is a measure of how confident you are in the underlying assumption, if no action is taken.

Urgency This is the date by which you need to start taking action in order to prevent the risk impacting. This is not normally the date on which the risk will impact (unless the action plan is very short and the risk will impact tomorrow) and is intended to build in the lead time required to manage the risk. So, for example, if the risk would impact in three months' time and the risk plan will take up to two months to complete, then the urgency date is one month from today. However, if the risk is two months away from impact and the risk plan could take three months to complete, then the urgency date is 'now' – indicating that you need to start taking action now, and you may already be too late. If you are very unsure of the time required to execute the risk plan, and this is very common just after the initial risk analysis, then the default urgency date is 'now'.

Note that criticality, controllability and urgency are intended as 'top-down' ratings in assumption analysis that senior management apply. The sensitivity and stability ratings on the assumption are bottom-up ratings that are applied by the team members being interviewed and they 'own' these ratings. This means that senior management cannot change sensitivity and stability ratings but they can apply criticality, controllability and urgency ratings as a way of correcting misperceptions of senior management strategy and priorities by the team members. This therefore 'levels the playing field'.

Risk profiles – bubble diagrams

Having prioritised your risks by criticality, controllability and urgency, you can further prioritise them into a descending list in a risk register. However, getting a true picture of priorities is only really possible with a picture and the bubble diagram is a very powerful way of seeing all the risk priorities on a single page.

An example of a RAG bubble diagram is shown below.

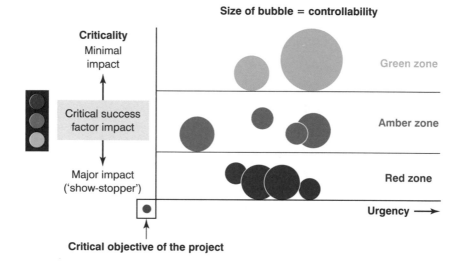

Plot each risk as a bubble. The colour of the bubble relates to its criticality. The size relates to the controllability, where large bubbles are difficult to control (i.e. C or D controllability) and small bubbles are easier to control (i.e. A or B controllability). The bubble is then placed on the x-axis based on its urgency. The origin (i.e. the intersection of the criticality and urgency axes) represents 'now' and 'showstopper' impact so that the worst case is a large red risk sitting at the origin. 'Bad' risk profiles have risks clustering around the origin while 'good' risk profiles have lots of space around the origin – see the figures opposite. Therefore senior management can quickly see projects that are under control and those that are out of control.

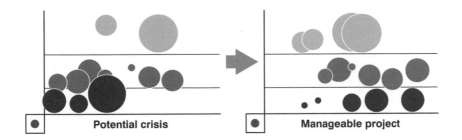

Potential crisis   **Manageable project**

The actual priority order of the risks is determined by the risk (bubble) proximity to the origin. Therefore in a risk review meeting, the first risk to be reviewed is the one nearest the origin; the next is the next closest and so on.

It is important to note that the criticality of the risk should be based on the 'worst case' impact. This should also take account of the compound effects of risks so that, for example, if three Amber risks could in fact act together to become a 'showstopper' then they should all be rated as Red risks.

Project prioritisation

If you are a programme manager, a portfolio manager or in any way responsible for a number of projects or business processes, the first step to effective risk management is to prioritise your projects to ensure that you allocate resources appropriately. Make sure management sees risk in an overall enterprise context.

QUICK TIP PROGRAMME VS PROJECT
A programme is not just a big project. A programme is a collection of interrelated projects that together will deliver defined benefits. Programmes are therefore significantly riskier than projects due to their complexity.

If you fail to prioritise and try to apply formal risk management to all projects equally, you will end up spending a lot of time and effort on projects that do not justify formal risk management approaches. This will also compromise your effectiveness in dealing with the projects that do need this degree of formality by spreading your resources too thinly.

Organisations often have a basic process for prioritising projects or processes but this is normally flawed as it is based on the value or cost of the project alone. This is clearly an important factor but does not take into account the benefits that should be realised or the chances that the projects will fail. For this reason you should prioritise your projects in terms of business criticality and complexity.

Business criticality This is effectively a measure of how much the business would suffer if the project failed to deliver, i.e:

→ A = little or no impact on the overall programme/enterprise if the project fails to deliver its objectives

→ B = manageable impact on the overall enterprise if the project fails to deliver its objectives

→ C = significant impact on the overall enterprise if the project fails to deliver its objectives

→ D = critical impact on the overall enterprise if the project fails to deliver its objectives.

Impact in this context should look at the ultimate benefit to the business and not just the money lost if the project fails. Also, small projects that could have a high strategic impact would rate as Cs and Ds. Similarly a small pilot project that may lead to a large programme could be rated a much higher criticality than it would if rated against pure size.

Complexity This is effectively a measure of the inherent risk in the project, for example:

→ A = simple project/processes/technology/ relationships *and* small team

→ B = complex project/processes/ technology/ relationships *and* small team

→ C = simple project/processes/technology/ relationships *and* large team

→ D = Complex project/processes/technology/ relationships *and* large team.

Note that complexity is strongly driven by team size. This is because small teams that are collocated tend to communicate directly, informally and effectively, whereas large teams that are spread around the organisation rely more on technology, particularly email, that is open to misinterpretation and misunderstanding. Miscommunication is the root cause of so much risk.

When plotted on a prioritisation matrix as below you can see clearly where management attention should be directed.

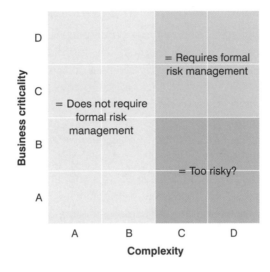

Organise a workshop of senior stakeholders and focus them on positioning their projects on this matrix. Projects on the left-hand side are not complex enough to justify the overhead of sophisticated risk management processes. That is not to say that you have no risk management of projects in this area – more that processes should be relatively simple. Projects that are positioned in the top right-hand quadrant are the ones that justify and need a formal risk management approach. Projects that are placed in the bottom right-hand quadrant raise some interesting questions: why as a business are you doing projects that are quite risky (and therefore likely to fail) but actually deliver very little business benefit? This matrix has in fact been used to effectively prioritise projects in a general sense, i.e. not just for risk management, so that decisions can be made regarding project approval, resourcing and even cancellation.

CASE STORY *POST-MERGER OPERATIONAL PRIORITISATION, PETER'S STORY*

Narrator Peter was the Global Operations Director for a newly merged bank.

Context After a tough merger integration programme, the newly merged bank was set new and very aggressive objectives.

Issue Following a largely successful merger integration programme, the bank effectively slipped back into ongoing operations relatively smoothly. The problem was that no evaluation had been done of which processes and projects were actually relevant to the new merged bank strategy.

Solution Peter instigated a formal project and process prioritisation exercise, executed across the global operations. This showed that many of the processes and projects were not providing a sufficiently positive impact on the business to be justified. In addition, some of these processes were leaking costs and some of the projects were inherently complex and therefore risky. Consequently, many projects were cancelled and business processes shut down without any noticeable impact on operational quality but with massive cost savings.

Learning The strategy of any business changes naturally over time and it's important to check periodically that your business processes and change projects are still aligned with your strategy and contributing sufficiently to support their continued existence. Prioritisation is a very high level and cost-effective way of evaluating the risks to the business.

5 RISK Governance

Project governance is the glue that makes the project successful. In its broadest sense it includes all processes that are employed, one of which is risk management. However, there seems to be a general feeling that the governance of risk management is 'obvious' and therefore doesn't require rigorous definition. This tends to lead to all kinds of problems, from taking little or no real action to manage risks, to risk management becoming a massive overhead as it balloons into a project in its own right. Optimise risk management governance so that 'it does exactly what it says on the tin'.

Risk registers

The risk register is the traditional 'list' of risks, normally appearing in priority order. The key to an effective risk register is to summarise at the right level so there is sufficient information for the reader to understand the risk clearly, why it is important, what the root cause is and what is being planned to manage it. Avoid the opposite extreme as well, where so much information is provided that no one can be bothered to read it.

Maintain and update the risk register on an ongoing basis. It should be a dynamic document from which reports can be produced to enable senior management to oversee, access and manage the risks. An example of the contents required in a standard risk register is shown below. Note that this example uses ABCD assumption analysis so the risks (the first line underlined in each group) are actually the 'risky assumptions' and are therefore positive rather than negative statements. The second line is the reason for the sensitivity rating (e.g. the immediate impact on the sub-project) and the third line is the ultimate impact (e.g. the impact on the overall project or programme). The fourth line, in bold, is the reason for the stability rating and is therefore the underlying concern or root cause of the risk.

Risk control

It's very common, when using traditional risk management, to expend lots of effort on risk identification and analysis and then very little real effort on actual risk control. Whilst it could be argued that the act of raising awareness through risk identification/analysis could help to avoid risk, there is no escaping the fact that most risks will require specific actions to be performed which are currently not planned in order to stop the risk occurring. Therefore you could also argue that risk management without explicit risk control is a waste of everybody's time.

Assuming that you overcome this hurdle, the next common problem with traditional methods is the tendency to produce unfocused and therefore wasteful risk plans. For example, it is not unusual to find a risk plan that attempts to reduce the impact, reduce the likelihood of occurrence and provide fall-back or contingency plans all in one go, when one of these would have been sufficient and far more cost-effective.

In ABCD assumption analysis, the focus on sensitivity and stability helps you to produce specific, cost-effective risk plans – see the figure below.

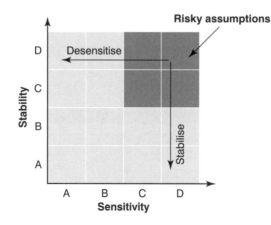

Look at the potential objectives of any risk plan and you can see that, with assumption analysis, there can only be two objectives. You can either:

→ **stabilise** the assumption, i.e. take some action to make the assumption more likely to hold, or

→ **desensitise** yourself to the effects of the assumption, i.e. make the assumption matter less.

Stabilisation risk plans tend to involve actions such as:

→ escalating to senior management to get their approval

→ achieving formal agreement with your client

→ getting two disagreeing parties together to gain consensus

→ securing resources that were under threat

→ changing policy to allow the preferred approach.

However, in general, stabilisation will require some form of **escalation.**

Desensitising risk plans tends to involve:

→ changing the overall approach

→ changing the plans to take the activities (that are underpinned by the assumptions) off the critical path

→ adding new resources (possibly with new skills) to the team

→ agreeing a relaxation of a milestone (although this also will change the planning baseline so, once it's agreed, the assumptions and/or their ratings may change).

However, in general, desensitisation will require some form of replanning.

Optimising risk plan objectives

You may be tempted when looking at the sensitivity/stability diagram to think that the ideal position to get to is 'AA' but this would probably be overkill and wasteful. An assumption ceases to be at risk when its sensitivity or stability is reduced to B, *in the eyes of the assumption originator.* Therefore your risk plan objectives should be to either stabilise *or* desensitise (but not both) to reduce from D or C to B. If you achieve A with no additional effort then that's fine, but additional effort to get from B to A is theoretically unnecessary. Practically, stabilising is normally easier than desensitising (e.g. it would take much less effort to get agreement from senior management than it would to replan the project). So, you should look to stabilise first and, only if that fails, consider desensitising.

Structuring risk plans

Risk plans may be anything from a single action to a detailed mini-project in their own right. Generally, risk plans need a few people to conduct a few steps. The key is to be specific in terms of:

→ what you are trying to achieve (i.e. the risk plan objectives)

→ how you are going to achieve the objectives (i.e. what the steps are)

→ who is responsible for performing the steps

→ when each step needs to be completed by.

There may be other things that you wish to capture, as in the example below, but this is the minimum set.

Risk escalation

Escalate a risk when it meets the following criteria:

→ the risk has a potential impact higher up the organisation (and even on the overall business strategy)

→ the risk potentially impacts other projects or business areas to a significant degree

→ you cannot manage the risk at your level in the organisation.

In ABCD assumption analysis, the basic escalation rule is to escalate all risks with a criticality of Red and controllability of C or D (i.e. the critical risks that are not under control). Any risks that are not rated as critical (i.e. Ambers and Greens) are unlikely to be of interest at the next level in the organisation. Similarly, any risk that is being effectively managed at your level (i.e. A and B controllability) would potentially waste management time if escalated.

QUICK TIP RISK ESCALATION
Only escalate risks that are critical and cannot be managed fully at your level in the organisation.

6 RISK Roles and responsibilities

Risk roles and responsibilities is another one of those areas that receives very little thought in most business environments or projects. Traditionally the roles are restricted to:

→ the risk manager: the person who is responsible for the process and, sometimes, for managing all the risks

→ the risk owner: traditionally the person who is totally responsible for the risk, once allocated.

These roles can create great confusion as:

→ the traditional risk manager cannot manage the risks by themselves – in most situations, they do not have the insight, the power or the resources to implement and follow through on risk plans

→ the traditional risk owner role encompasses responsibilities that are in conflict, i.e. it is very rare that the right person to own the risk is also the person who is in the best position to action the risk.

For these reasons, the roles in ABCD risk management are defined rather differently. For each risk, allocate two roles:

1 **Risk owner.** This will be a senior manager who is in the best position to understand and assess the risk and therefore also best able to assess when the risk has been sufficiently managed. This person must also be a member of the committee that review risks (e.g. the 'risk review board'). The risk owner is the person who would suffer most if the risk impacts and is therefore motivated to make sure that the risk action manager follows through on the risk plan.

2 **Risk action manager (RAM).** This will be the person in any part of the enterprise who is in the best position to take action to manage the risk. This person could be on your team or on someone else's team (including the customer's team). They could be below the risk owner in the organisation, at the same level or even in a superior position (e.g. if the action required is to gain agreement at a senior level in the customer organisation, then this is the only way that the action is likely to be successful).

 QUICK TIP RISK OWNERSHIP AND ACTION
Ownership and action are very different responsibilities. For each risk, assign a separate risk owner and risk action manager.

Roles are normally allocated on a very logical basis. For example, if the assumption is: 'The design specification will be signed off by 1 May' and this is at risk because the project funding is still not agreed, the risk owner is probably the design manager (i.e. suffers the immediate impact) and the risk action manager is probably the finance manager (i.e. to clear the funding).

Set up a **risk administrator** to run the process. This is a similar role to the traditional risk manager role but it is totally focused on the efficient running of the process and should not involve content (i.e. the risk administrator could only be a risk owner or risk action manager if the risk is related to the risk process itself). Also avoid using the term 'risk manager' as this reduces any preconceptions and avoids any confusion with the risk action manager.

The relationships between the roles is shown in the diagram below.

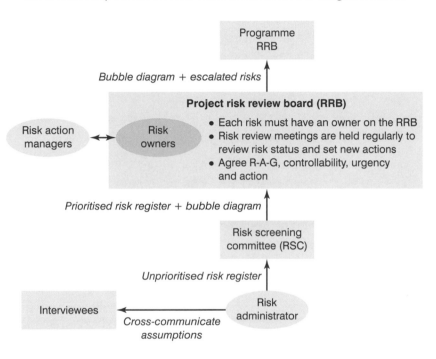

Risk review boards

The traditional risk meeting is very often known as a 'talking shop' where senior management could spend an hour discussing one risk and still not be sure that anything tangible will come of it. This situation is even worse if you have 50 risks on your risk register that will probably never get discussed.

For these reasons, the ABCD risk review board (RRB) was designed as the focal point of the risk management process and is an action-oriented way of reviewing, prioritising and following through on risk plans. The key points and processes are:

→ **RRB membership**: The membership of the RRB will typically be the same as the senior management team meeting but ensure that every risk has an appropriate risk owner (i.e. someone who understands the risk and can assess the status of the mitigation plans). Occasionally it will be necessary to 'co-opt' someone on to the RRB to be a risk owner while a particular risk is active. Therefore the membership can and will change over the life of the project or programme.

Select your membership based on getting the right balance between people who understand the risks and senior management (in order to make things happen). The members of the RRB will be the risk owners and so, looking at the initial risks, you should ask yourself the question: 'Who do we need to be able to discuss these risks appropriately?' Risk action managers do not need to attend the RRB but some risk owners may be RAMs on other risks.

For example, if there are 30 risks in the risk register – 10 impact on design, 12 on testing and 7 on roll-out and 1 on financing – you will probably need the design manager, the test manager, the roll-out manager and the finance manager as potential risk owners at the RRB. If any of these managers are fulfilling a purely administrative role (i.e. they don't understand the technicalities of the risks) then use the person on the team who does understand the risks as the risk owner (e.g. the design architect may attend the RRB instead of, or as well as, the design manager). Also, when the finance risk is resolved, the finance manager can stop attending.

→ **Frequency**: RRBs are normally held on a monthly basis but may be more frequent if the status of the programme dictates. To ensure momentum and follow-through on actions, it is unusual for the frequency to drop below once a month.

→ **Before the RRB meeting**: it is the responsibility of risk owners to review their risks before the meeting and to ensure that they fully understand the risks, agree with the ratings and are clear about any actions underway. For new risks it may be necessary for the risk owner to communicate with the assumption originator (if the risk owner did not originate the assumption) to make sure that they fully understand the risk and underlying drivers. The risk owner should also consider what actions will be required and who would be the best person to undertake those actions (i.e. the risk action manager). For ongoing risks the risk owner will need to get an update on the risk plan status from the risk action manager.

→ **During the risk review board**: discuss the risks in **priority** order as indicated by the bubble diagram (i.e. those nearest to the origin first). The process for each risk should be:

  → The risk owner should **clarify** the risk briefly (if necessary).
  → The meeting will endorse or change the **ratings** for criticality, controllability and urgency.
  → For new risks, suitable (high-level) **action**(s) will be agreed and a risk action manager will be assigned or agreed to develop the risk plan.
  → For existing risks, the risk owner will **report** on behalf of the risk action manager (unless the risk action manager is present) on the mitigation progress, and when the risk is considered as resolved the risk owner will agree the **closure** proposal. (Note that the risk is not formally closed in the risk register until the assumption originator agrees to downrate or close the associated assumption. This ensures the integrity of the process by stopping senior management overriding the team's viewpoint.)
  → At the end of the meeting there should be time to raise any urgent assumption/rating queries and discuss them as risks, if appropriate.

→ **After the risk review board**: update the risk register and bubble diagram from the meeting and reissue to all risk owners as a formal record of the meeting and actions agreed. Risk action managers are then responsible for undertaking the actions agreed in risk plans while risk owners are responsible for making sure that actions are followed through (by the risk action manager) in a timely fashion.

For projects and programmes that have a large number of risks outstanding (say more than 50) it is often useful to constitute a risk screening committee (RSC) prior to the RRB. The RSC has two primary roles:

1 As a sanity check. Does the risk make sense? If it doesn't, go back to the assumption originator prior to the RRB or temporarily remove it from the risk register until it is clarified.

2 To undertake a preliminary assessment of the criticality and controllability ratings. The ratings are not formalised until the RRB has endorsed or changed them.

The idea of the RSC is to reduce the 'administrative' burden from the RRB and allow board members to focus more on mitigation. In order to undertake this assessment the RSC is typically made up of the risk administrator and at least one member from the RRB.

Hierarchical RRBs and risk escalation

In a large project or programme, the RRBs can be layered so that, for example, several project RRBs feed into a programme RRB. In this situation, the risks are identified in two ways:

1 Programme risks, identified by focusing, top-down, on the critical assumptions that need to happen in order for the programme to deliver its benefits.

2 Escalated project risks that meet the escalation criteria, i.e:

→ the risk has a potential impact higher up the organisation (and even the overall business strategy)

→ the risk potentially impacts other projects or business areas to a significant degree

→ you cannot manage the risk at your level in the organisation.

Alternative RRB structures

For projects where a relatively small number (say less than ten) are involved in the assumption capture process, it is practical to hold a RRB with all assumption originators present (which may be all ten people but no more). This meeting should concentrate on agreeing ratings and allocating RAMs and reports to a more senior risk meeting to ensure that actions are being followed through.

The advantages of this approach are that the discussion of risk is all first-hand and it is not necessary to hold a RSC prior to the RRB. The disadvantages are that the meetings tend to be long as there are more things to discuss, and this format becomes impossible in larger programmes and projects because the number of people required to be present becomes impractical.

 CASE STORY *BPO OUTSOURCING PROGRAMME, CLARE'S STORY*

Narrator Clare was commercial director involved in a major business process outsourcing deal.

Context The deal involved considerable legal changes in order to take over the staff of the client's organisation.

Issue Many of the legal issues had never been addressed before due to the 'novel' nature of the deal. Added to this, the programme deadlines were necessarily aggressive in order to realise the benefits of the deal.

Solution Clare instigated an ABCD programme risk management process that included quality based costing analysis of both cost and timescale risks. The timescale risk assessment showed her that the deadlines were being seriously threatened by one of the legal/ commercial agreements required. Clare had no prior experience of this and quite rightly estimated the timescales required for agreement with a high degree of uncertainty. This was the only Red 'showstopper' timescale risk identified for the deal programme. Initial reaction from senior management was to seek more information to see if Clare's viewpoint was appropriate. Whilst management were probably correct to approach the risk in this way, communication delays resulted in three weeks being lost before the risk was reassessed and the reassessment was that it would take even *longer* than Clare had indicated. One week after the reassessment, the deal collapsed as there was no way of meeting the deadlines required, i.e. the risk was realised.

Learning Once you have a risk process that you have confidence in, you must trust the views of the stakeholders who have input to it and act on their views appropriately and quickly. Risks often have a very urgent nature and only by acting quickly can you hope to resolve them. On a positive note, the analysis was proven to be accurate – there was one showstopper and it did ultimately stop the show!

7 RISK Trends

'You can't manage what you can't measure' is a common mantra. It might be true, and spotting risk trends can tell you something about your strategic risk profile that you will never see by looking at the individual risks.

Bubble diagram trends

The bubble diagram provides an effective way of getting a quick overview of the risk profile without going into the details of the risk register. Each bubble represents a risk and the colour corresponds to the criticality. The size of the bubble relates to the controllability of the risk. The urgency of the risk is indicated by the bubble's proximity to the origin. Overall, space around the origin is good and clustering around the origin is bad.

As a snapshot in time this is useful but display the snapshots over time and you will see if risk management is really working. In the example opposite, the first two diagrams indicate considerable risk but each subsequent month shows improvements that would suggest that the project will ultimately be delivered successfully.

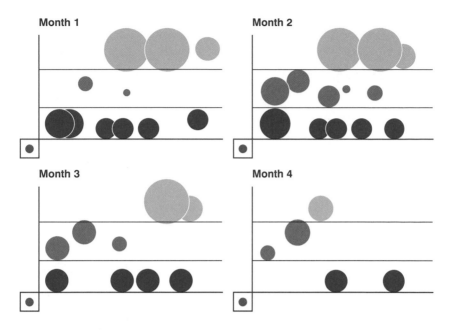

Alternatively if the trend is as below, the implication is that the project is failing and will never be delivered by trying to tactically manage each individual risk. In these circumstances, take a step back and look for fundamental strategic underlying causes and, if in doubt, be prepared to stop the enterprise while you find them.

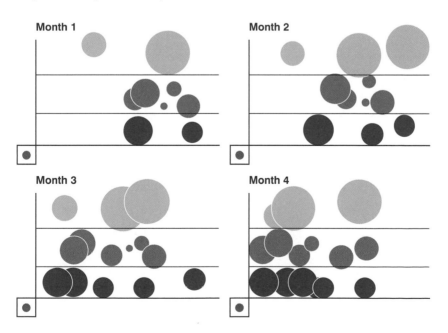

Don't panic after your first analysis when the profile will almost inevitably be 'bad'. Watch the trend over the next two to three months before drawing conclusions about the likely success of the project based on this analysis. Allow time for the risk plans to take effect. It is common for the start of the analysis to show two or more months of the profile getting worse before improvement.

Risk drivers

Risk drivers are, not surprisingly, designed to categorise the underlying 'driver' of the risk. The idea is to identify trends in the drivers over time that either confirm anticipated patterns or alert you to fundamental problems that may require strategic solutions.

For each risk, identify the underlying driver and allocate it to one of:

→ **milestone** – where the driver is due primarily to time pressures

→ **technical** – where the primary driver is due mainly to the complexity of the enterprise or technical problems.

→ **policy** – where the driver is primarily due to 'politics' (e.g. company policy, decisions required, more resources).

For example:

→ **'XXX will be completed by 31 April'** and the underlying concern is that 'previous experience suggests that 50% more time will be required'. Driver = milestone.

→ **'XXX will be completed by 31 April'** and the underlying concern is that 'it uses new technology that is new to the company'. Driver = technical.

→ **'XXX will be completed by 31 April'** and the underlying concern is that 'we need sign off of the purchase order to engage YYY resources'. Driver = policy.

This example shows that the risk driver may not be obvious from the risk or assumption statement and it is normal to need the underlying concern to identify the driver correctly.

Once you have a significant number of risks (say 40) to analyse, undertake a risk driver analysis. Plot the percentage of risks that fall into each category (i.e. milestone, technical, policy) over time (e.g. at the end of each month). The 'normal' distribution for a typical (successful) project should be as shown below.

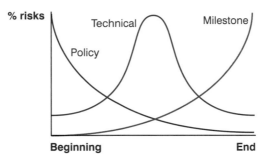

The basic logic is as follows:

At the **beginning** of the project you would expect:

→ a high percentage of policy risks as there are normally lots of decisions to be made at this stage

→ a very low percentage of milestone risks as the team should be feeling relatively relaxed about timescales

→ a low percentage of technical risks as the solution is rough and detailed problems and concerns are yet to emerge.

In the **middle** of the project you would expect:

→ a low percentage (and falling) of policy risks as these should have been substantially resolved by now

→ a low but slowly rising percentage of milestone risks as time pressures increase and interim milestones become imminent

→ a high percentage of technical risks as the design is completed and (theoretically) all of the technical issues are identified.

At the **end** of the project you would expect:

→ very low (if any) policy risks as these should all be resolved by now

→ a high percentage of milestone risks as it is natural for teams to feel the time pressure as the final deadlines get closer

→ a low percentage of technical risks as these should now be substantially resolved.

If your profiles vary significantly from these profiles, then be prepared to dig deeper.

→ A high percentage of milestone risks at the start of the project may mean that the timescales are not achievable.

→ A high percentage of technical risks at the start of the project may mean that the solution is fundamentally flawed.

→ A high percentage of technical risks at the end of the project could indicate that design issues are being carried over into implementation and then show up in later test phases.

→ A high percentage of policy risks at the end of the project may indicate that the project is heading for trouble due to outstanding decisions not being made early enough.

→ A low percentage of milestone risks at the end of the project may indicate that the timescales are too relaxed and should be tightened.

Use these trends as guidelines only and take account of what is specifically happening in your project or programme. Sometimes you might see one of the trends that normally indicate trouble, but there may be some event in your project that explains the trend (e.g. change requests, interim milestones, design reviews) and therefore you do not need to be overly concerned.

However, if the analysis still looks worrying, then you must look for strategic rather than tactical solutions. For example, if the percentage of technical risks are rising towards the end of the programme, then there is little point in trying to manage them one at a time – there is probably a design fault that needs to be resolved and therefore it will be more effective to stop the programme and undertake a design review.

QUICK TIP RISK TRENDS
Looking for risk trends over time can identify strategic risks that trying to manage risks one by one will never fix.

8 RISK Metrics and Behaviour

Give your team the best risk process and toolset on the planet but don't forget to give them a little 'push' to make sure that they use them effectively.

Minimise administration

The simple truth is that people will not embrace a management process unless they get significantly more out of it than they have to put in. If the team thinks that the risk management process is for the benefit of senior management or audit/compliance, members will participate but they will do the minimum they can get away with, effectively 'ticking the boxes'. Convince the team members that risk management will make their jobs easier and more effective, and there's a good chance they'll do it well.

Risk management generates the most value if it is continuously helping management and team members to identify risks that they hadn't previously thought about and then guides them through efficient risk mitigation – see the figure below.

Most risk management processes fail in both these regards, i.e. they get people to log risks that they are already aware of and even risks that they are already actively managing. People then consider risk management to be a waste of their time. Very often the risk is already known but the tendency is to accept, ignore, transfer or insure the risk even when direct mitigation might be a good option. Also, there will be risks that people are unaware of and then are affected by, when they would have been able to control the risk relatively easily if it had been identified earlier.

The ABCD assumption analysis process is a good example of a process that deals with this problem. ABCD helps to identify the risks that would never be identified by traditional means by forcing the cross-communication of assumptions and their ratings. ABCD also guides people through mitigation by focusing on the stabilisation or desensitisation of the underlying assumptions.

Set up risk metrics

It is very difficult to measure the effectiveness of risk management. Its probabilistic (i.e. multiple possible outcomes) nature means that you can never be sure that the action that you took did actually stop the risk occurring since it may not have occurred anyway. However, what you can measure is how well your team is performing in the risk management process. Set up metrics to measure elements such as:

→ **Time open** – for each risk, to see where risks are not being followed through to closure.

→ **Average time open** – this should be measured for risk owners and will drive them to close down risks as soon as possible. Provided you are using a robust process, like ABCD, they will not be able to close the risk without agreement from the assumption/risk originator and so they cannot force inappropriate closure.

→ **Actions overdue** – this should be measured for risk action managers to indicate who is keeping up with their allocated actions and who isn't. As soon as an individual action in a risk plan goes past its planned closure date without it being completed, the whole risk plan should be flagged as overdue.

These metrics should be used both to praise and to 'name and shame'. Provided senior management are keeping up with their actions, the team will follow their lead and a significant shift in behaviour should be seen within two or three monthly cycles.

Treat these metrics as guidance only. For example, don't be harsh on the risk owner of a risk that has a naturally long risk plan. However, if this risk is discounted from the individual's metrics and the person is still performing poorly on all the other risks that they own, then feel free to put the boot in good and hard.

Reward positive behaviour

Having established metrics to measure individual performance of risk management, link these measures into an individual's performance evaluation. People are used to being evaluated on things like revenue, profit, team management, marketing, etc. but it is almost unheard of for risk management to be one of the criteria used.

It is therefore not surprising that people treat risk management as non-essential and something to do when you have time for it. If targets are set for risk metrics, as above, then immediately this becomes a performance measure that they can ignore at their peril and you will naturally drive them to prioritise risk management higher up their 'to do' list.

> **QUICK TIP ENCOURAGING RISK MANAGEMENT BEHAVIOUR**
> Make risk management effectiveness a formal performance evaluation criterion for your team.

9 RISK And groupthink

When groups make decisions, they may well take more risks than the individuals themselves would – this is 'groupthink'. The psychologist Irving Janis coined the term in the 1970s. Janis defined groupthink as a phenomenon where people seek unanimous agreement in spite of contrary facts pointing to another conclusion. Groupthink tends to occur when a group strives to reach consensus despite the fundamental concerns of the individuals, combined with a high degree of homogeneity of members' social backgrounds and ideology. Extreme pressure or stress exacerbates the situation.

Symptoms of groupthink risk

Whenever you are in a group environment there are eight symptoms of groupthink risk to look out for:

1 **Illusions of invulnerability** creating excessive optimism and encouraging risk taking.

2 **Ignoring warnings** that might challenge the group's assumptions.

3 **Unquestioned belief** in the morality of the group, causing members to ignore the consequences of their actions.

4 **Stereotyping** those who are opposed to the group as weak, evil, biased, spiteful, impotent or stupid.

5 **Direct pressure** to conform placed on any member who questions the group, couched in terms of 'disloyalty'.

6 **Self-censorship** of ideas that deviate from the apparent group consensus.

7 **Illusions of unanimity** among group members; silence is viewed as agreement.

8 **Mindguards** – self-appointed members who shield the group from dissenting information.

If not addressed, these symptoms can lead to:

→ an incomplete survey of objectives

→ an incomplete assessment of alternatives

→ failure to examine the risks of the preferred choice

→ failure to re-evaluate previously rejected alternatives

→ poor information research

→ selection bias in collecting information

→ failure to work out contingency plans.

Examples of groupthink disasters

Recent examples of business groupthink disasters would be Enron, Northern Rock, Lehman Brothers, RBS and HBOS. In HBOS a well-publicised story circulated about the risk manager who was 'censored' for raising concerns regarding the company's strategy.

However, much of Janis's research was based on a series of US foreign policy disasters in the 1970s and, in particular, the Bay of Pigs fiasco. In 1961, approximately 1,400 Cuban exiles, helped by the US military, were landed on the coast of Cuba at the Bay of Pigs with the intent of overthrowing the regime. Within three days virtually all were dead or captured. President John F. Kennedy approved the invasion based on advice from a 'team of experts'. The team made a number of key assumptions that proved to be false, including:

→ the invasion will trigger an uprising amongst the Cuban population – it didn't

→ there will be no requirement to retreat from the Bay of Pigs after landing – there was; and so on...

Janis concluded that the group of experts did not consider alternative viewpoints on the invasion sufficiently and fought too hard to achieve consensus. JFK accepted their conclusions because they were 'experts'. Interestingly, when the Cuban missile crisis developed, JFK managed the situation very differently.

Another classic example of groupthink risk was the Challenger space shuttle disaster in 1986. Against the recommendations of individual engineers, the 'group' agreed to launch and we all know what happened next. In records of meetings leading up to the launch, there are numerous examples of ignored warnings, stereotyping, direct pressure and ultimately silence being viewed as agreement.

Avoiding groupthink risk

There are a number of relatively simple but effective ways of avoiding groupthink from an organisational perspective.

(Tip)

QUICK TIP AVOID GROUPTHINK

→ Use external experts to challenge the group's thinking.

→ Set up multiple groups to work on the same issue.

→ Appoint a 'devil's advocate' for key meetings to test conclusions.

→ Ensure that senior management avoid expressing opinions before key meetings/projects.

When JFK was faced with the Cuban missile crisis in 1962, he seemed to have learned well from the Bay of Pigs. During planning meetings, he invited outside experts to share their views, and allowed group members to question them thoroughly. He also encouraged group members to discuss possible solutions with trusted members within their separate departments, and he even divided the group up into various sub-groups, to break down the group cohesion. JFK was deliberately absent from the meetings, so as to avoid pressing his own opinion. As we know (because we are all still here), the Cuban missile crisis was resolved peacefully, and the role of these measures has since been acknowledged.

How does ABCD help to avoid groupthink?

When ABCD was originally developed in 1992 it was specifically tailored to avoid the problems that are frequently encountered with traditional risk management techniques. Groupthink was one of the problems considered and is addressed by:

→ **Interviews** – workshops are a terrible way of capturing risks where the group dynamics will allow certain individuals to dominate the discussion while others remain quiet. Interviews ensure that all voices are heard equally and are significantly more efficient than workshops for risk identification.

→ **Assumptions** – by focusing on positive assumptions rather than negative risks, all aspects of the enterprise are considered in a positive and systematic way and openness is naturally encouraged. People are led to think about what needs to happen for success (i.e. the assumptions) rather than being forced to look for failure (i.e. risks), which is psychologically unnatural.

→ **Assumption ratings** – ABCD operates on a 'worst case wins' basis, i.e. the person who is most concerned controls the ratings even if they have isolated views. This forces people to communicate so that the minimum risk plan is to force the 'optimist' to talk to the 'pessimist'. This will either resolve concerns or identify risk that the majority had missed.

→ **Top-to-bottom integrity** – senior management can set overall risk ratings (i.e. criticality and controllability) but they are not allowed to change assumption ratings or close risks/ assumptions. Risks can only be closed when the assumption originator agrees to downgrade the ratings.

So would the use of a technique such as ABCD have prevented the Challenger shuttle disaster? Who knows, but the rigorous structure that ABCD imposes would certainly have ensured that all assumptions were evaluated appropriately for risk by all key players before the launch was sanctioned.

 CASE STORY *THE CHALLENGER SHUTTLE DISASTER*

Context Space shuttle launches had become commonplace by the mid-1980s and each launch was driven by more and more commercial pressures.

Issue The Challenger launch had been delayed several times already and the bad publicity was creating pressure in addition to the 'normal' commercial imperatives.

Solution The day before the launch, the project senior management team met to agree an appropriate go or no-go decision for the launch. Several of the engineering team were concerned that the 'O-rings' on the rocket boosters would be out of specification if the weather forecast for the following morning of freezing temperatures was realised. The engineering team subsequently recommended that the risk would be too great to launch before the temperature had risen back into the specified range. The problem was that the current weather forecast showed that the temperature might not reach that range for some weeks. The management team put pressure on the engineers to reconsider:

→ 'The shuttle has been launched 19 times without a problem.'

→ 'Take off your engineer's hat and put on your management hat.'

→ 'OK, so we will launch as scheduled – does anyone have a different position?'

The decision was taken by the group to go ahead despite the fact that several individuals still thought that the risk was too great.

The O-rings failed and Challenger with all its crew was lost.

Learning Groupthink can creep into any organisation and many examples of disasters since Challenger have been attributed to groupthink, including the subsequent Columbia shuttle disaster.

Particularly when commercial and timescale pressures are high, take a step back and ask yourself if the risks that have been identified by individuals are being squashed by the group and be prepared to stand firm. If necessary, quote the examples of groupthink disasters to make your position stronger.

10 POSITIVE APPROACHES To risk management

Risk management can be seen, quite understandably, as a negative subject. Although there are many subtle ways of dealing with this potential problem, there are also some overt techniques to enthuse your team.

Opportunities

On the surface, risk management seems to be all about avoiding 'bad things'. When implemented fully, risk management should also address realising 'good things' in the form of opportunities. Gamblers understand this duality of risk very well. If they lose, then this is the threat that they accepted by gambling. If they win, then this is the 'upside risk', the reason they play the game.

The benefits of extending risk management to include opportunities include:

→ **Formalising the capture and management of opportunities**. By utilising systematic capture, analysis and follow-through, opportunities that would have been either completely missed (or achieved by luck) will be realised in a rigorous fashion.

→ **Engagement of the team**. Individuals who may be less than enthusiastic about risk management will probably be significantly more enthusiastic about opportunity management with its positive connotations.

→ **Offsets risk**. In any venture, some risks are going to happen. However, if some opportunities are also realised, then this might offset the risks and bring the enterprise back on course.

→ **Accelerates implementation**. If taken to its ultimate conclusion, the systematic management of opportunities can result in projects being implemented earlier than originally planned, for less than their original budget and even delivering more than was promised.

Most risk management methods and guidelines now recognise both the threat and opportunity sides of risk but they vary enormously as to how to integrate these two opposites into one methodology. In ABCD, the focus on assumptions (i.e. the things that need to happen in order to meet your objectives) tends to mean that the balance between risks and opportunities is even. Thus the assumption is that what you need to happen in order to meet your objectives and the impact of the assumption proving wrong could be either positive or negative. Depending on which way this goes, rate any 'risk' that emerges as either a risk or an opportunity.

Risk =

Red =

→ 'showstopper' i.e. critical project objective not met (e.g. deliverable, milestone, budget, reputational)

→ unacceptable cost impact to business

→ no possible or acceptable contingency plan.

Amber =

→ significant objective not met

→ significant cost impact to business

→ difficult contingency plan.

Green =

→ minor or localised objective not met

→ minor cost-impact to business

→ contingency plan identified and acceptable.

Prioritise a Red opportunity (i.e. too good to miss) the same as you would a Red risk. At the end of the day, one may cancel out the other.

Opportunity =
Red =

→ critical improvement on objectives

→ save time by a critical degree

→ massive cost-saving opportunity

→ critical opportunity to enhance reputation.

Amber =

→ significant opportunity to exceed objectives

→ significant time-saving opportunity

→ significant cost-saving opportunity.

Green =

→ minor or localised opportunity to exceed objectives

→ minor time-saving opportunity

→ minor cost-saving opportunity.

Selling risk management

Selling the benefits of risk management can be tough. You need to overcome the perception that risk management is an administrative overhead by making sure that it is identifying and managing risks that would not have been identified without the risk management process. But even then, you cannot *prove* that a risk did not happen because of the risk management process – it is a risk and therefore there is a distinct possibility that it would not have happened if no action had been taken at all.

It helps to have lots of examples where risk management has delivered significant benefits but there is also a simpler way to convince people. Ask your team/management/customer if they think that it is likely that at least one 'showstopper' will be identified by the use of a formal risk management process. Unless the venture is relatively small, it is highly likely that they will realise that something significant is going to be missed without a formal risk management process. Identifying one showstopper risk will probably cover the costs of implementing and running the risk management process many times over. If the venture is small and simple, then formal risk management probably can't be justified anyway.

Joint risk management

It is very common for significant projects or programmes to be pursued with the supplier and customer (and even third-party suppliers) using different risk management processes. While you may think that it is good that they are all doing something about risk management, the use of different processes can cause specific problems of their own.

The primary problem is that the processes tend to be developed and used in isolation. This means that risks are identified from different perspectives, with different priorities and with different risk plans. This leads to completely different perceptions of risk and can make things look far more risky than the true picture, due to the inevitable misunderstandings and miscommunications in any complex business venture.

For example, I was recently involved in a large outsourcing programme which was perceived to be coming off the rails. The new contractor was fairly confident of meeting the migration date but the incumbent contractor was lobbying for cancellation of the programme (because they were genuinely concerned based on their risk assessment, not just because they were the incumbent contractor). The client didn't know what to make of the situation (based on their risk assessment) and so the project's destiny hung in the balance.

We implemented a common ABCD based risk management process focused on capturing and cross-communicating the key assumptions – see the figure opposite. The initial analysis, which just covered the contractor (see 1 September) showed a much riskier picture than they anticipated. By the time the client and incumbent's assumptions had been included (see 23 September), the risk profile appeared to confirm the incumbent's original view. However, you should never panic after the initial assessment as you don't know how much this is real risk versus perceived risk. And this proved the perfect example of this phenomenon.

The true risk profile was probably revealed by the fourth risk review board on 22 October. By this point the communication between stakeholders had been driven through, all parties were in agreement that what was left were indeed the real risks, rather than just misunderstandings and miscommunications. The client was encouraged to proceed based on the obvious improvement in the risk profile between the 23 September and 22 October. By 16 November the risk plans were progressing well and working, and carried on through to 9 December where the go/no go meeting had to basically decide if the two 'showstoppers' were likely to be managed. The go ahead was given and the day before the migration weekend, it was agreed by all parties that all significant risks to the programme had been mitigated. The reality was that the migration weekend went off without any significant issues and the system went live again on the Monday without any users being aware of what had happened – until they were formally notified. All parties agreed that this would not have been achieved without joint risk management.

 QUICK TIP *PERCEIVED RISK VS REAL RISK*
It is quite normal for there to be a significant difference between the risks as initially perceived and the 'real' risks. Formalised communication between stakeholders will close this gap.

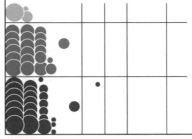

1 Sept
Contractor only view

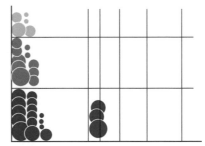

23 Sept
All stakeholder view

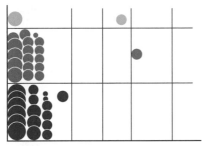

29 Sept
All risk plans in assure

22 Oct
Real risk revealed

16 Nov
Mitigations effective

30 Nov
Almost there...

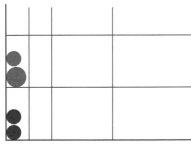

9 Dec
Go/no-go meeting

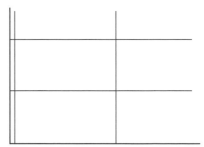

17 Dec
Day before migration weekend

CASE STORY *BANK MERGER PROGRAMME, TONY'S STORY*

Narrator Tony was head of IT and Operations for a newly merged global bank and a key stakeholder in the subsequent merger integration programme.

Context The merger integration programme was separated into the regional areas of the Americas, Europe and Asia.

Issue Most senior management discussions focused on the problems in Asia despite the fact that Asia was the smallest part of the merged bank's business. The Asia management team were very good at 'shouting the loudest' and it was working.

Solution Tony formally prioritised the merger projects around the globe using ABCD and this showed that the Asia project portfolio was generally low down the list of priorities. He linked this into the ongoing ABCD programme risk management process by defining the risk rankings of Red, Amber and Green consistent with the project prioritisation. In this way, 'minor' projects were unable to raise Red risks by definition and most of the Asian projects were capped at Green when looked at from a global perspective. This meant that no matter how loud the Asian management team shouted, the formal Global Risk Review Board could give appropriate attention to all risks across the global programme.

Learning Ultimately the exercise that Tony undertook proved to be very valuable. It was realised that, in order to meet the minimum set of critical objectives for the merger by the deadlines, in the worst case Asia could be left out completely. This allowed management to focus on the right risks in the right order and not be distracted by 'noise'.

Clarifying the 'risk' in risk management

Professor Chris Chapman Emeritus Professor, University of Southampton, School of Management

A common, but simplistic, definition of 'risk' is 'risk = probability × impact'. However, this definition seriously distorts productive

EXPERT VOICE

thinking about risk. Its focus is events. It cannot address uncertainty involving ambiguity about objectives, alignment of objectives, incomplete design information, systemic uncertainty/risk and other issues that really matter. There is a good case for arguing that the corporate failure of Railtrack in the 1990s was a consequence of managing rail safety using this approach. The basis is expected 'equivalent fatalities' per annum for railway systems and this clearly needs minimisation, but large deviations from what happens on average drive public perceptions of railway risk and railway management competence.

Risk management cannot be undertaken without reference to performance objectives of some kind. Defining objectives for particular performance attributes affects the nature of associated risk. For example, setting a difficult to achieve 'tight' budget for a project makes the project more risky by definition, in the sense that the chances of exceeding the budget are increased. Conversely, setting an easily achievable 'slack' budget makes the project less risky because the chances of exceeding the budget will be decreased. Consequently, selecting relevant performance attributes, formulating objectives for these attributes and modifying objectives, should be regarded as important, even fundamental aspects of risk management.

Start by thinking about uncertainty about *your* objectives. What are your objectives? Use a suitable level of decomposition from broad aims. Some objectives will involve measurable attributes like 'revenue'; others will involve non-measurable attributes like 'customer confidence'.

Then think about three 'performance levels' for each performance attribute, starting with a key measurable performance attribute. One performance level is 'S', a 'stretch target' – a plausible 'no problems' goal to aim for if you are lucky and exploit all your opportunities. Another is 'C', a 'commitment value' – a performance level you can sensibly commit to, bearing in mind you may be unlucky, the trade-offs involved in making 'C' too low or too high, and any exclusions (scenarios involving outcomes you will not take responsibility for). A third level is 'E', an 'expected value', and your estimate of what will happen on average. Setting 'S' as an optimistic outcome with, say, a 90 per cent chance of not being achieved, and 'C' as a pessimistic outcome with, say, a 90 per cent chance of performance better than this, then E can be approximated by $(S + C)/2$. Your 'provisions' for uncertainty are the differences between S and E values – on average you will need them. Your 'contingencies' are the differences between C and E values – on average you should not need them.

Now think about 'risk' as possible downside (threat side) deviations from suitable performance levels for each performance attribute. For many

EXPERT VOICE

purposes, E is a suitable performance level. In a safety context, S = zero might be appropriate for some purposes – zero 'equivalent fatalities' from no serious accidents is the stretch target, and 'risk' includes any serious accidents. In some contexts, including safety, setting a commitment level C might be appropriate – where the chance of performance worse than C is small.

Next think about decomposing overall views of uncertainty associated with each performance attribute into sources of uncertainty for estimation and option choice purposes.

Until 2007, the Highways Agency used a common practice project risk management approach to cost major road projects. Uncertainty about costs was quantified by a focus on possible adverse events described in probability and impact terms. An inevitable consequence was that costs were consistently underestimated and projects were high risk in cost terms. A report to the responsible minister[1] suggested changes to this approach[2] which satisfied all concerned. A key part of the changes was recognising that engineers' initial estimates needed three somewhat different provisions. One was for uncertainty associated with basic costing assumptions, a second for 'risk events' in the usual sense, and a third for changes in scope due to quality improvements driven by changes in EU safety rules and comparable Highway Agency policy decisions. All three are essential to produce an estimate appropriate for ministerial use, and the second is usually the least important.

Risk management is a risky business. It is particularly risky if all the relevant parties do not have a shared view of what risk means and whose risk is being discussed.

[1] Nichols, M. (2007) *Review of Highways Agency's Major Roads Programmes: Report to the Secretary of State for Transport*, Nichols Group, London.
[2] Hopkinson, M., Close, P., Hillson, D. and Ward, S. (2008) *Prioritising Project Risks: A Short Guide to Useful Techniques*, Association for Project Managers, Princes Risborough.

4

TECHNOLOGIES

To remain as effective and efficient as possible, FastTrack risk managers differentiate themselves by the support mechanisms they put in place to help themselves and their team. This includes the intelligent use of appropriate information technologies – enabling, for example, the automation or semi-automation of administrative activities thereby freeing up time to focus on managing risks and motivating and leading the risk team.

Getting started

Why consider technology?

Risk management is one of those activities that can accumulate a lot of data. Whilst this is useful for audit and compliance purposes, it is not much use for actually managing risks unless the information is accessible, visible and effectively communicated.

In fact a critical success factor in risk management is to ensure that data is effectively communicated around the stakeholder group. Once stakeholders are fully aware of the assumptions that are being made and the perceived risk to those assumptions, there is a good chance that the risks will be managed or avoided altogether.

In essence the use of technology is all about enhancing visibility and control. Visibility means getting the assumptions/risks in front of the people who need to know. Control means providing a mechanism to plan and manage risks and ensure follow-through.

QUICK TIP *LATEST TECHNOLOGIES*
Take time once a quarter to review the latest technologies, and look for ways to improve the effectiveness of your team.

What activities should we focus on?

Before deciding how to use technology or automation to save time, eliminate entirely low-value or unnecessary activites.

Start by making a map of the current risk process, and then make a list of all the current risk management activities across the team. Then assess how much time and resource is spent on each activity and the value you associate with each one – perhaps using a simple four-point scale. Draw a simple two by two matrix to assess where each activity falls on the scales of 'Time spent on the activity' and 'Value the activity adds' – see the figure below.

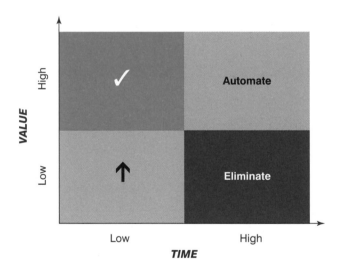

→ Those activities falling in the bottom right-hand corner are the critical ones to address – high time but low value. Try to eliminate these. For example, perhaps you are spending a significant amount of time during each weekly or monthly review deciding if concerns are actually issues or risks. Set up a screening mechanism to review these concerns before senior management get involved and apply clear criteria – e.g. 'issues' have already become problems and 'risks' have not yet happened but have the potential to become issues.

→ Those activities in the bottom left-hand corner pose a problem. They are not consuming much time, so are reasonably efficient, but they are not delivering a lot of value. Perhaps there is a way of improving the value of each activity. You might, for example, change the agenda on a risk meeting to use time more efficiently.

→ Activity in the top left box are already efficient and of high value. Perhaps they are already automated, so leave them until your next review.

→ There will of course be risk management activities that make a big difference but are time-consuming in terms of compiling risk registers, cross-communicating assumptions/risks, compiling reports for risk meetings and ensuring that actions are followed through. These are by definition important and high value, so you do not want to get rid of these activities, but you need to find more efficient ways of doing them.

Think carefully about your overall time management: be aware of how you use your time and constantly look for ways of improving this. Once you have formally conducted a time–value assessment, you will be more conscious of this need. Don't forget that we tend to do those things that we enjoy and put off what is less fun. If you're serious about putting technology to the best possible use, then try to overcome this psychological bias and look at the use of your time as objectively as you can. If you do not manage your time well, you will find it difficult to fit the risk management task in because it doesn't impact your short-term objectives – risk management is the classic 'not urgent/important' activity.

In general, when invited to meetings, constantly ask the question 'Why should I go?' What value will the meeting give me, or what value will I give to it? If there is no obvious answer, then decline the invitation, or delegate. The key is to remove unnecessary tasks and activities before looking for opportunities to automate: that way you avoid putting IT and other resources into something that has little or no value.

Finally, encourage your team to carry out the same exercise so that when you are deciding on various options for automation you are aiming to increase the overall effectiveness of the team, not just yourself.

The process-system link

How should we use information technology?

Think carefully about how you will use technology and ensure it links back to what you are seeking to achieve. Perhaps the starting point is to look at your overall risk management framework and look for opportunities to make each element quicker, simpler and possibly more fun.

Some aspects of the framework will lend themselves to the use of technologies, whereas some of the softer areas such as leadership and culture will offer fewer opportunities.

Make sure that the information provided is accurate and timely so that you have the confidence to act on it. Think carefully also about security; who will be using the technology, what information will it contain and how sensitive is the data? Most technologies are becoming more secure but you need to take time to ensure you set them up correctly in the first place, and that you have the appropriate level of security.

Top technologies

How do I know what technology exists?

Having understood the need for technology, systems and automation and where you are going to deploy technology for best effect, how do you find out what is available?

Get into the habit of scanning for technology trends on the Web, in industry journals or at trade fairs and exhibitions. Look at what other people in your business are reading – particularly those you most admire. Where do they get their information? Take time to find out what other firms, perhaps your competitors or suppliers, are using.

However, be aware that there is a lot of information available, and there are new technologies coming along all the time. How do you decide what is relevant and what is useful? Make sure you start with a healthy scepticism. Investigate the technology, but ask the 'So what' question: Is this relevant to my team and to me and how will it impact performance?

What tools will support a sustainable approach to risk management?

Recognise that the development of technologies is moving so quickly that the list of what is available to you will never be static. Use the following list as a challenge to what is possible, but accept that it is a snapshot of what is happening at a point in time. The key is to get into the habit of constantly scanning this field in search of ideas for improving the effectiveness and efficiency of your risk framework. The following list summarises the main options that are available today along with their pros and cons.

QUICK TIP *SEARCH THE INTERNET*
Schedule a monthly half hour to search the internet (e.g. search on 'risk management software') for potential sources of ideas and information and make a list of the top five websites to monitor on a regular basis, or set up Google alerts.

1. Risk register spreadsheet

What is it?	Most people will recognise this as a 'default' tool for organising and sorting data.
Pros	Relatively simple to access and configure. If you already have a package such as Microsoft Office then Excel will be bundled and therefore effectively 'free'. This is a simple solution for a small project risk register.
Cons	The reconfigurable aspect makes it virtually impossible to impose any standards – people will want to add new fields. This makes aggregating information, for example from projects to programmes, very difficult. Effective communication is extremely difficult as you will either need to send around a 'master' spreadsheet or lock down the master in an e-room that may be seldom visited.
Success factors	For small ventures/projects, spreadsheets provide an easy and effective medium. Spreadsheets are not suitable for larger projects, programmes and enterprise solutions.

2. Risk database

What is it?	A formal software tool that allows the input and extraction of data that is held in preset fields.
Pros	Relatively easy to set up. A typical database package such as Microsoft Access will do the job and is relatively inexpensive.
Cons	Has to be held as a centralised resource or on a (locked-out) network which compromises communication. Often needs specialist database package knowledge to reconfigure and change reports.
Success factors	Use an easily accessible database (ideally on your company intranet) for relatively small projects/ventures. Not really suitable for larger projects, programmes and enterprise use.

3. Risk web-based tool

What is it?	An internet-based tool that allows input and output of data via a browser.
Pros	Input and output from anywhere by anyone with internet access (via password control). Collaborative online working possible. Easy access tends to encourage communication. Flexible security arrangements possible. Scalable to any size of enterprise.
Cons	Probably the highest cost option.
Success factors	Best option for large projects, programmes and enterprise risk management solutions.

4. Blog

What is it?	Personal accounts of processes, experiences, references, etc.
Pros	Useful to keep abreast of latest thinking in risk management. Occasionally may find free risk tools to download.
Cons	Almost always linked to a commercial organisation, so recommendations will probably be biased towards their products. Free tools are probably over-simplistic or a 'lite' version of products that you have to pay for.
Success factors	Useful for latest thinking. Simple tools will be suitable for simple projects.

5. Social media

What is it?	Internet-based networking sites such as LinkedIn, Facebook, Twitter, StumbleUpon, Digg, etc.
Pros	Useful for connecting with like-minded professionals and keeping up with the latest thinking – note social media is moving increasingly into the business arena. There is also potential with Twitter to create a 'closed' system for communicating information around the business.
Cons	Can be time-consuming to filter out the 'noise' and get to the value.
Success factors	Useful for latest thinking. There is considerable business potential in social media that is likely to become mainstream in the next few years.

What it really boils down to is 'horses for courses'. There is probably no point in investing in a sophisticated web-based tool for managing risk on a small project where a risk spreadsheet will suffice. However, if you have a large portfolio of projects, or a large programme, then a web-based tool will probably be justified and may, through effective communication amongst stakeholders, prevent anything from a snag to a catastrophe.

You cannot effectively run a risk management process on a large project or programme with a risk spreadsheet. Many have tried and many have failed. The logistics of updating data, passing it around the project and producing effective reports is likely to prove so onerous as to compromise communication and hence the risk management process. This is where a web-based tool really comes into its own and is worthy of deeper review.

QUICK TIP USE APPROPRIATE TECHNOLOGY
If you have a portfolio of projects, prioritise them and use simple risk spreadsheets for risk management on small projects, reserving web-based tools for the larger/ complex projects.

Considerations for web-based toolsets

Not all web-based tools are made equal. The one thing that they all do is to enable real-time access to data from anywhere (via an internet connection, of course). There are many further aspects that you should consider if you are in the market for a web-based risk management tool.

→ **Security** – If you are undertaking a joint risk process with your customer/suppliers it is likely that you will want to control access of data so that some is shared and some is private. Most tools will have at least two levels of security: the first to log on to the site and the second to log on as a specific user. The user's profile should then automatically restrict the user to the data that they should be able to read and change.

→ **Complexity** – Tools can have very complex functionality but this should only be visible to those who need to be aware of it, such as 'administrators'. The average user will not need to access all the functionality, and over-complexity can be a deterrent to use as people may feel intimidated by the technology. Effective web-based tools often have the facility to direct users to different home pages depending on their profile. This means that administrators get full functionality whereas senior managers, by going to their own or the appropriate home page, may be given limited options (e.g. only to access their own risks and print a risk register).

→ **Flexibility** – Some tools are going to be generic and complex so that you select the fields that you want to use and ignore the ones that you don't want. This gives an 'off the shelf' approach but can be limiting, particularly in terms of reporting. The alternative approach is to customise the tool to your specific requirements. To be able to do this, the tool must be very flexible otherwise the costs and timescales for customisation will be prohibitive.

→ **Reports** – All tools will come with a standard set of reports (e.g. risk registers). With some tools, additional reports can be specified and paid for as a change request. The best tools have report functionality that can be configured by trained administrators or even users, without the need for any detailed technical knowledge.

→ **Scalability** – Projects typically require a single database of risk data. Programmes of interdependent projects require layered information at programme and project level and perhaps even sub-project level. Enterprise risk management requires a much more sophisticated structure and layering with the ability to filter and sort out appropriate information.

→ **Escalation** – Linked to scalability is the ability to escalate appropriately between levels in the programme or enterprise. This can be automatic (setting fields causes immediate escalation), semi-automatic (setting fields alerts administrators that escalation is required) or totally manual (administrators decide what to escalate and when). Experience has shown that a semi-automatic escalation is likely to work best on any significant sized venture.

→ **Triggers** – Linked to escalation is the ability to trigger 'alerts' on significant changes of status – see the figure below. For instance, if an action in a risk plan is not completed by the agreed date, the action could be automatically set to 'overdue' and perhaps an email alert sent automatically to the risk owner. Triggers can be very important in changing and driving behaviour related to action follow-through.

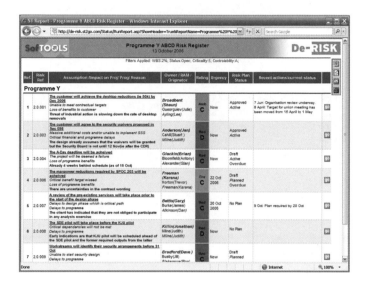

→ **Dashboards** – Some ability to maintain an overview of risk status is very important to 'see the wood for the trees'. This can be anything from a breakdown of number of risks open in each project to an automatic generation of some graphical overview (e.g. a bubble diagram) – see the figure overleaf.

→ **Process** – Last but certainly not least is the fact that the tool will be ineffective if the underlying risk management process is inadequate. Sadly, many web-based tools have simplistic processes that allow poor-quality data to be entered and analysed. This effectively leads to GIGO (garbage in, garbage out) where no matter how sophisticated the tool is, its impact on real risk management is minimal.

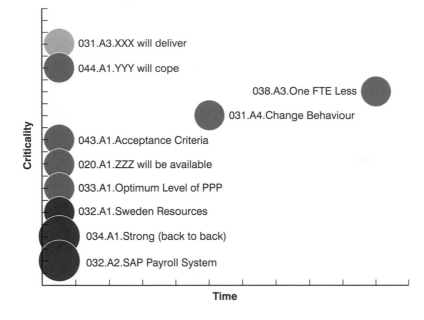

How do I keep balance?

Now stop. Before going out and investing in the latest and greatest software tools, remember that technology is just an enabler. Success will ultimately depend on your ability to lead others, your behaviours and how you interact with others.

Be wary of being drawn into new technologies too quickly – let someone else make the mistakes, but then learn quickly

Finally, if you do decide to introduce new systems into your team, think carefully about the possible risks: what assumptions are you making and what could go wrong?

✋ **STOP – THINK – ACT**

Ask yourself and the team these questions:

What should we do?	What technologies are available that will help to improve effectiveness and efficiency?
Who do we need to involve?	Who would benefit and why?
What resources will we require?	What level of investment would be required?
What is the timing?	When would be a good time to introduce the new technology – is there a 'window of opportunity'?

Visit **www.Fast-Track-Me.com** to use the Fast Track online planning tool.

In the following expert voice, the expert discusses the merits of traditional financial valuation models and presents an alternative approach to evaluating future options and scenarios. Again, the assumption based method for risk management used in combination with these approaches can provide an advantage to the forward-thinking manager.

💬 **Real options and scenario planning: an integrated approach to investment risk management**

Professor Giampiero Favato Kingston Business School, London

EXPERT VOICE

❝❝ Managers tend to make the same kind of decision-making mistake, referred to as 'frame blindness', i.e. setting out to solve the wrong problem because a mental framework has been created for a decision that causes the best option to be overlooked. In fact, the word 'option' is extremely relevant because in recent years practitioners and academics have argued that traditional cash flow models do not capture the value of all the options embedded in many corporate decisions. These options need to be considered, because their value can be substantial.

Deterministic models, such as the discounted free cash flow valuation (DCF) tend to overlook the strategic reason for an investment, such as investing in a marginally profitable project in order to acquire future growth opportunities. In conditions where technology rapidly becomes obsolete, investments may be made for competitive reasons alone and such investments may well fail the DCF test.

DCF fails also to take account of the value added by active management. Management has to decide when to invest, how operating plans should be modified during the life of a project and whether to abandon a project in midstream. By guiding a project from beginning to end, management may be able to squeeze its cash flow distribution towards a higher than expected rate of return. This has led to the development of the idea that because management control can impact upon a project's payoff, control opportunities can be seen as being analogous to 'call' and 'put' options and they may be analysed using option pricing theory. Like DCF analysis, the real options perspective involves projecting future cash flows and choosing an appropriate discount or volatility rate. However, unlike DCF analysis, the real options perspective assumes managers can influence the outcome by making a series of successive decisions which add value over time.

Scenario planning encourages managers to envision plausible future states and consider how to take advantage of opportunities and avoid potential threats. Through scenario planning, contingencies, uncertainties trends and discontinuities that are often unanticipated can be identified. While scenario planning is primarily a qualitative method of analysis used to identify risk, when combined with the real options approach it takes on a more quantitative identity, able to be used effectively in assessing value creation under conditions of uncertainty. Eventually, quantitative values have to be assigned to the probability and impact of each scenario on the critical factors determining the investment's payoffs.

The merit of this integrated approach to risk is appealing: while scenario planning turns managers' attention toward the external environment, an assessment of potential real options available provides an effective tool to evaluate the possible responses and create value from uncertainty. The combination of the two types of analyses constitutes an integrated decision-making process for management and it yields changes in the way management approaches strategic decisions. It makes strategy an evolutionary process, flexibly moving from one choice point to the next through time and creating a new 'space' for decision-making choices.

INTEGRATED RISK MANAGEMENT PROCESS

Step one	To create scenario 'plots' of future sales of the business, where managers identify where each business is exposed to three levels of environmental contingencies:
	→ general uncertainties (macroeconomic, social political, natural)
	→ industry uncertainties (market, product, competition, technological discontinuities)
	→ company uncertainties (operations, credit, R&D, liability, human capital).
Step two	To identify exposures and the relative investment options to maximise the value or hedge risk.
Step three	To evaluate investment alternatives using real options analysis.

EXPERT VOICE

5

IMPLEMENTING CHANGE

There is no one right approach to the creation of a sustainable approach to risk management. Decide for yourself what is and is not appropriate for your business and team, think ahead and plan the changes carefully.

Whether implementing risk management for the first time or changing processes and toolsets, this is a change programme in itself. Therefore you need to address the 'softer' aspects of getting buy-in from your team (and possibly customers and suppliers) as well as rolling out the process and tools.

Planning the way ahead

At your first planning meeting with your team, look at each of the key building blocks for putting your risk management framework in place. If the gaps are still unclear or you are seeking to make your business 'world class', then use a structured audit based on the risk management maturity model in the directors' toolkit.

For most new risk management champions, this first planning meeting will generate a significant number of areas that you will want to change but you can't do everything at once; so identify the key areas to focus on. The following example may be wider than you can (or want to) handle at the moment, but it illustrates what happens when a risk management champion tackles the whole topic of an integrated risk management framework. Depending on your circumstances, you may only be able to handle parts of such an implementation.

Imagine that in the initial meeting you have identified the following aspects of your risk management framework that your team feels represent the greatest opportunities for improvement:

→ **Identification of risks is sporadic and inconsistent.** Risks are not identified systematically as the templates used are not completed properly, not completed on time or not completed at all. Perhaps you require a workshop or interview-based risk identification.

→ **Prioritisation of risks is poor/inconsistent.** Impacts of risks are not considered in balance, with too much emphasis on financial impacts (e.g. contractual penalties) and not enough consideration of softer impacts (e.g. reputational impact). Perhaps you need different scales and ways of looking at prioritisation in a more holistic way.

→ **Escalation of risks is poor/inconsistent.** Risks are frequently escalated to senior management when they shouldn't be and there are several instances of risks not being escalated that should have been. Perhaps you need to formalise the rules for escalation and even automate them in some way.

→ **Risk meetings are unstructured, poorly attended and unproductive.** Meetings are held infrequently, undermining the effectiveness of the risk management process. When the meetings are held, they tend to take a long time and very little is formally agreed. Risk owners fail to follow through on their allocated responsibilities, leading to ineffective risk plans. Perhaps a review of the roles and responsibilities is required, with particular reference to the role of senior management in making the risk process work.

→ **Spreadsheets used to capture and disseminate the risk register are frequently amended inappropriately.** Merging of spreadsheets from each sub-project is difficult and time-consuming. Perhaps a more robust tool is required to smooth the administration and improve communication of risks around the business.

> ### QUICK TIP ASK 'WHY?'
> Get into the habit of asking 'Why?' Why is this process the
> way it is, why do we have to do things this way?

Great ideas for improvement, but how do you start to implement them? Clearly these changes are significant and it would therefore be unwise to just do it without a lot of thought but, at the same time, you need to get on and these ideas might provide an opportunity for you personally to make an impression on your senior management. It is vital that implementing these changes goes well.

You will need to: set the team up to maximise its potential to succeed; create an effective implementation plan; and avoid the typical pitfalls associated with implementing change.

Making a plan

How should we introduce changes?

So, you're on your way to implementing your risk management framework. There's one thing for certain and that is that people will have to accept changes to the way they do their job now. Such change is painful for many, almost impossible for some but – the good news – some people who want to take their team, organisation and careers forward will welcome change for the better.

The first step is to involve all the stakeholders at an early stage. Make a complete list of who they are and then prioritise them using the diagram overleaf.

You would like to have all stakeholders on board but you must try to get the key stakeholders in the top right-hand quadrant (i.e. S1 and S2) to be reasonably supportive of the changes required.

To achieve this, first talk to your strongest supporters who have influence (i.e. S3, S4 and S5). You could include S7, S8 and S10 in these discussions if convenient, but this is not essential. Try to understand from this group why they support the initiative and how they, or you, might 'sell' this viewpoint to the other stakeholders. Next have one-to-one meetings with S1 and S2 to fully understand their concerns, find out what it would take to make them supportive (or at least neutral) and, perhaps, explain why other stakeholders are supportive. Be very careful with this last point as you need to balance confidentiality, avoid conflict and make sure that the next stage (if required) has the desired effect. With luck you will find that the S1 and S2 stakeholders have a misunderstanding with what you propose. You can deal with that rapidly in the one-to-one sessions.

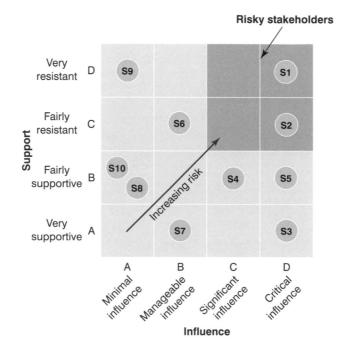

The next stage, if still required, is to get all the key stakeholders together. Explain what you are trying to do and restate clearly what the potential benefits to the organisation are to maximise chances of getting buy-in. Open up the discussion to give people the chance to air their concerns. If issues you were expecting do not get raised, raise them yourself – you do not want stakeholders to suggest agreement by silence and then raise issues again outside and after the meeting. If your supporters are not forthcoming in their support when you expect it, then gently prompt them. When all the aspects that should have been discussed have emerged, ask the key question: 'So are there any significant concerns remaining why we should not go ahead with the initiative?' Silence at this stage is good.

Before ending the meeting you must agree responsibilities for the stakeholders and immediate next steps. Do not let the people leave the room before this has been achieved, including when this group (or a subset of it) will meet again to assess progress.

QUICK TIP *REMOVING BARRIERS*
Take time constantly to look at your part of the business and ask, 'What are the barriers to effective risk management?'

Next you need an implementation plan. Work out what your objectives are carefully. Ask yourself how you will know that you have succeeded in creating a sustainable approach to risk management and give yourself a realistic but stretching time target to get there. Make sure the boundaries within the objectives are clearly stated so that you avoid the possibility of 'scope creep,' an inherent 'risk' in any fundamental change to the organisation. For example, suppose you're trying to get the company's strategy clearly articulated. Scope creep would mean that you start to do the articulating yourself, risking setting out the definitions of the strategy independently of the senior managers responsible for the strategy. Your objective is to get the people responsible to articulate the strategy.

Once you have the objectives, you're in a position to make a list of the activities involved in achieving them. Take time to identify ownership, timing and resource requirements, asking what is necessary for success.

For example:

Project: implementing your new risk management system

Phase 1: Improving risk identification and analysis

Activity 1.1: Replace templates by interviews and workshops for risk identification – design and train team.

Activity 1.2: Set up new way of prioritising risks based on 'total business impact'.

Activity 1.3: Design a new way of escalating risks with a view to semi- or total automation.

Phase 2: Improving risk planning and follow-through

Activity 2.1: Set up a new governance meeting (i.e. risk meeting) focused on validation, rating and risk planning/follow-through.

Activity 2.2: Research and implement a new risk management software package that reduces administrative overheads.

You may want to break these activities down further but don't over complicate the plan and make planning an overhead itself.

At the end of each phase of your implementation, stop and formally assess performance – these review points, called milestones, allow you to check that you have achieved what you set out to achieve. Now look at a timeline and produce a Gantt chart showing what is to be done and by when. Below is an example based on the topics at the start of this chapter.

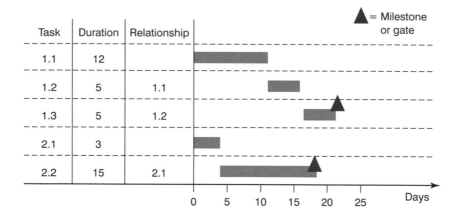

It may be that you can implement other elements of your risk management framework with informal meetings with the management team and specialists within market research. Remember, an implementation plan can be very useful, but some activities are straightforward enough not to need detailed documentation.

So, you now have an outline plan of how to implement a company-wide (or division-wide or just for your team) risk management system, the time has come to get everyone to buy in to the plan by communicating it to all the stakeholders. Avoid surprises wherever possible, so involve key people early in the planning process. You can do this with a conference or a series of emails. You may need a newsletter, but recognise that it takes time and skill to get this right. Don't do newsletters too frequently or you'll find that there is nothing this month really to report. Eventually you'll find that the flow of information about the framework will be one of the most important roles the risk management champion has.

One essential requirement is to practise what you preach. In this case it means that you must risk manage the implementation. You can't hope to get buy-in to a new risk management process if the implementation goes overdue, over-budget or fails to meet key objectives *and* particularly if there was no formal risk management of the project. In fact this is a great opportunity to show how effective the new risk management system could be.

QUICK TIP *APPLYING RISK MANAGEMENT TO YOUR IMPLEMENTATION PROJECT*
Practise what you preach – apply the new processes to the implementation project and deliver on time, to budget and meet all key objectives.

You'll need a budget and resources. Work out what ideally you will need: remember that you will have to give a justification (i.e. a business case) for the expense and the resources. It's probably not sufficient to say that without a new risk management process the organisation will 'die'. You need more specifics and you need to relate the business case to the achievement of business goals. Look for success stories from companies that have done it before. Point to things that have gone wrong in the past and how much they have cost the company. Look for quick wins – simple things you can do either before you get your new budget or things that you can do quickly afterwards. Make the quick wins as concrete in financial terms as you possibly can.

Ensuring success – keeping the plan on track

What approach should I use? The 'plan-do-check-act' cycle

Now you have to keep the project plan on track. Simply putting a plan together does not mean it will happen. Think about the three Ps that you will need to manage – plan (tasks and timings), people (keeping stakeholders motivated and on track) and performance (the project objectives) – and keep your attention balanced on all three.

The PDCA cycle – see the diagram opposite – is a continuous improvement approach to managing a project or team. Use it as a structured approach to monitoring performance and progress, and for remaining alert to the unexpected.

→ **Plan** your activities – you will have done this already if you have a Gantt chart like the one above.

→ **Do** implies completing the activities necessary for success.

→ **Check** the progress you're making towards implementing the plan. This means capturing the key assumptions that you are making in the plans and assessing them for risk. This will reveal any potential problems in any of the three areas concerned. For example, 'suitable resources will be available for training in the new risk management process'. There could be a number of things that could stop this assumption being realised. Plan – a resource that you need may not be available at the time you had planned to have it. Can you change the plan so that the overall timescale is not affected? People – the implementation may go too slowly. Do you change the plan or bring in someone else to speed things up? Performance – a person you are hoping to train may not show the necessary interpersonal skills. Do you down-skill the role or try to replace them quickly?

→ **Act**, make decisions that will bring the project back on track by resolving the problems. Make sure that you do not try to fix problems that do not need fixing, i.e. apply the risk management approaches described in Chapter 3 and therefore make sure that you manage risk appropriately.

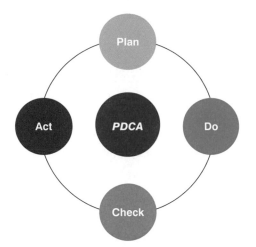

What routines should we set up?

Complex situations can be dramatically simplified through regular structured review meetings. Depending on what you are looking to achieve, these may be quick and simple five-minute updates by the coffee machine, or more in-depth, one-day workshops involving all key stakeholders. Reflect on all of your regular meetings:

→ daily, weekly, monthly – these focus on performance monitoring and risk/issue resolution

→ annual cycles (if appropriate) – these focus on strategic planning and priority setting.

How do we stay flexible?

Whilst you need to understand the principles of planning and performance monitoring, you also need to stay flexible and responsive to the team, aware of how things are going and changes in the external environment. Think about how tight or loose your controls really need to be. Too loose and you run the risk of missing deadlines and going off at a tangent, but too tight and you run the risk of reducing the team's motivation and losing key stakeholders' commitment.

Nowhere is this tight versus loose leadership style more visible than when a team leader or change project manager uses some of the tools and techniques of project management and gets bogged down by them. Take the example of critical path analysis: this is a useful technique that shows the leader and the team what activities are critical to the completion of the plan on time. You can afford other activities, ones not on the critical path, to slip a bit without compromising the end date of the plan. It's a useful guide for both planning the timing of activities and monitoring progress but it is only really useful for relatively large complex project plans. Don't get too carried away with it or you risk damping down the creativity of the team and causing motivation problems by an unhealthy concentration on the tasks as you planned them. Critical path analysis can be helpful but in the end it's the people not the tight process that will deliver the results you want. I have known situations where the project manager was so intent on ticking off the activities on the project network that people were ignoring shortcuts and better ways of doing things just to keep him happy.

QUICK TIP *DAY–TO–DAY ACTIVITIES*
Look for ways to build creative thinking into day-to-day activities – and also 'think risk'.

Balance the team's rational thinking with tapping into their creative talents. Encourage risk management even while you're involved in setting up a risk management environment. You will spot the people who will help more on one side of the rational/creative spectrum and learn to rely on the rational ones to keep the project steady and the creative ones, from time to time, to make a huge step forward. Some people go from one mountain top to the next one by plodding down the mountainside then plodding up the other one. Others prefer to take a leap and hope they make it. When they do, they have made a great contribution to the team; when they fail, you and the team will have to help them recover. It's the balance of the two that ensures not only success but also the best result possible.

STOP – THINK – ACT

What should we do?	What stages and tasks are appropriate?
Who do we need to involve?	Who needs to be involved and why?
What resources will we require?	What information, facilities, materials, equipment of budget will be required?
What is the timing?	How long will each activity typically take?

Visit **www.Fast-Track-Me.com** to use the FastTrack online planning tool.

In this next expert voice, the expert explores a potential link between operational risk management and project risk management. It is useful to recognise interrelationships, but at the same time it is often more practical to assess and manage them independently.

Operational risk and infrastructure

Professor Stephen Ward University of Southampton, School of Management

Professor Stephen Ward University of Southampton, School of Management

EXPERT VOICE

No longer is the public impressed with the physical manifestation of infrastructure. It is not the construction projects – roads, railways, airports, docks, water-mains, power stations, waste incinerators and so on – but the services they enable that matter to stakeholders. Increasingly, success is measured by an absence of major disruption to everyday life, and by major projects creating infrastructure assets that broadly deliver the operational performance that was forecast when their go-ahead was committed.

Operational risk is associated with uncertainty about the performance of infrastructure once it has been constructed, during the typically long-lived operating phase of infrastructure projects. Obvious sources of operational uncertainty and risk are future costs of operations, maintenance and administration, and levels of future use in rapidly changing social, economic and technological conditions. Risk also derives from impact upon stakeholders that force consequential major changes to operational practices and performance requirements. Then the financial consequences may be great and the impact upon operator organisations can be profound. One obvious prominent example of this is the commercial operation of the Channel Tunnel.

Operational risk associated with infrastructure can be a significant concern in several ways. First, the construction of major infrastructure assets usually involves the coincidence of three key features: high capital cost, long lives and costly post-construction modification. Further, the expected operating life is often unclear, although economic appraisals typically assume a minimum 15–25-year operating life. In making such investments, there is a need for early consideration of the operational stage in terms of its likely costs and benefits. In some cases, future operating costs (even after appropriate discounting) may substantially exceed the more immediate construction costs. Clearly, where the financial viability of projects is also dependent on future revenues associated with use of the asset (as in a toll road, railway, bridge, tunnel, power station, waste treatment plant or railway), then a good understanding of both future costs and revenues is critical.

Second, one-off events can occur during the operation of infrastructure that have a major impact on performance, with both immediate, short-term effects and longer-term effects through, for example, consequential responses and impact on operator reputation. The importance of operational risk related to particular infrastructure assets, or groups of assets, depends on the extent to which relevant stakeholders are affected. Localised effects of realised risk on infrastructure might be regarded as less significant than effects on the wider sector. However, localised effects may signal a need for a wider action to alleviate operational risk due to particular commonly occurring sources of risk or uncertainty. For example, investigation of the causes of a rail crash may suggest a need for a change in network-wide operating maintenance protocols, whereas vehicle collisions on a motorway usually do not.

Third, major operational risk can arise from cumulative effects. All operations encounter small-scale problems with relatively short-lived consequences, capable of being managed locally on a day-to-day basis. However, if not addressed in a timely manner, the cumulative effect of such problems can become significant: increasing inefficiency, increased costs, reduced staff morale and motivation, shifts in organisational culture, and changes in stakeholder perceptions of the infrastructure operator. Attendant consequences for the operator can include funding, regulation and revenue issues. Within infrastructure businesses, operational risk can readily escalate to become a strategic risk for the organisation.

Effective management of operational risk requires a holistic approach that recognises the linkages between operations, strategy formulation, and project management. For any infrastructure operating business, a risk assessment of existing operating assets needs to inform long-term strategy, which in turn drives individual projects. Operational risk is then managed on two fronts, one related to maintaining operational 'business as usual', the other addressing longer-term operational risk via appropriate strategies and intelligent design of new assets from an early stage in the associated project life cycles.

EXPERT VOICE

PART C

CAREER
FAST TRACK

Whatever you have decided to do in terms of developing your career as a manager, to be successful you need to take control, plan ahead and focus on the things that will really make a difference. You need to ask yourself how you get into your company's key talent pool.

The first ten weeks of a new role will be critical. Get them right and you will get off to a flying start and probably succeed. Get them wrong and you will come under pressure and even risk being moved on rather quickly. Plan this initial period to make sure you are not overwhelmed by the inevitable mass of detail that will assail you on arrival. Make sure that other people's priorities do not put you off the course that you set yourself.

Once you have successfully eased yourself into your new role and gained the trust of your boss and the team, you can start to make things happen. First, focus on your leadership style and how it needs to change to suit the new role; then focus on the team. Are they the right people and, if so, what will make them work more effectively as a project team?

Finally, at the appropriate time, you need to think about your next career move, and whether you are interested in getting to the top and becoming a company director. This is not for everyone, as the commitment, time and associated stress can be offputting, but the sense of responsibility and leadership can be enormously rewarding.

You've concentrated on performance up until now – now it's time to look at your Fast Track career.

6

THE FIRST TEN WEEKS

The first ten weeks of starting a new role as the leader of any team are probably the most critical – get them wrong and you risk failure, get them right and you will enjoy and thrive in your new role. What do you need to do, where should you focus, and what must you avoid at all costs?

To enable the new leader to take control, the Fast Track manager will seek to understand key facts, build relationships and develop simple mechanisms for monitoring and control – establishing simple but effective team processes. Again, this task will be simplified using modern technologies and so becomes effortless and part of day-to-day behaviour.

QUICK TIP RISK MANAGEMENT IS A CAREER ENABLER
A role in risk management will naturally give you access to all levels of the organisation. Get noticed (for the right reasons) and your career should take off.

Changing roles

Why is this a critical time?

Whenever you start a new role or job, whether within your existing business or joining a new company, you have an opportunity to make a positive impression on others. However, recognise that you will only get one chance to make a first impression[1] – get the first few months wrong and it could impact your relationships with others for a very long time.

During a period of transition, the team you will be joining will have few preconceptions. People will typically have an open mind and be willing to try new ideas, giving you the benefit of the doubt. We often see this phenomenon when consultants are called in to resolve a critical business issue. They often say exactly the same things as some of the internal managers, but as outsiders their views are respected and acted upon.

This is typically a period of high emotional energy, and activities will often get a higher level of enthusiasm and commitment. Use this time wisely and you will gain significant advantage.

What are the potential pitfalls?

Whilst this period of transition presents opportunities to make a good impression, take care not to get it wrong. Few people recover from a bad start in a new role. You will be faced with a number of challenges to overcome:

→ You may lack specific knowledge and expertise in your new role. This will make you vulnerable to making wrong decisions

→ In every team there will be a mixture of people and politics. Getting in with the wrong people or setting up favourites can limit your opportunities for future promotion.

→ There will be a lot to do in a short period of time, and you may well feel overwhelmed by it all.

→ Most effective managers rely heavily on their informal networks, but in the early stages of a new job these don't exist.

What is the worst-case scenario?

Because people often give the benefit of the doubt to those who are starting a new job or joining a new team, things often go well for a period of time. If you make mistakes they will forgive you because you're new to the job. This is referred to as the 'honeymoon period'. New

[1] Michael Watkins (2003) *The First 90 days*, Harvard Business School Press, Harvard.

football coaches, for example, are allowed to lose the first few games without too much criticism. However, after a period of time (the first ten weeks), you, like the coaches, will need to perform well, meeting the expectations of key stakeholders and winning.

During this initial period, it is vital that you take the steps necessary to set yourself up for longer-term success, or else run the risk of falling into the chasm[2] – see the figure below; you make a good start but then people start to see what you are doing as just another management initiative. Plan your first ten weeks carefully in order to set yourself up for longer-term success.

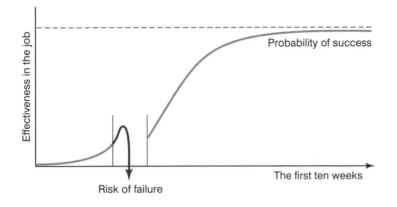

The first ten weeks

What should I do before I start?

This section looks at the first ten weeks from the perspective of a risk management leader (e.g. an enterprise risk manager, programme risk manager, etc). However, the steps would be the same for, say, a programme manager with significant risk management responsibilities, so read between the lines.

Before starting a new project or job within the area of risk management, you need to do your research in terms of what it will entail and what some of the potential problems are likely to be. Develop a personal to-do list of things to put in place.

[2] Adaptation of concepts presented in *Crossing the Chasm*, Geoffrey A. Moore (1999) Harper Business. Revised edition.

QUICK TIP TEN MINUTES OUT
Get into the habit of taking ten minutes out each day simply to browse the internet. Get to know your customers, competitors and emerging new techniques and technologies.

Think also about how you yourself will need to change. How will you behave differently, what knowledge will you need to gain and what new skills would be useful? Understanding these things will help to build your confidence.

If possible, it would also be useful to identify key influencers in the field of risk management such as industry experts or any internal experts, and start to build your reputation through your involvement in events or discussion forums.

CASE STORY GOVERNMENT CHANGE PROGRAMME – KARENA'S STORY

Narrator Karena was the new programme manager for the supplier of a major IT driven change programme.

Context A very large government change programme was underway to change the way the department worked with its key suppliers over the next ten-year period. The department's largest supplier, who was also acting as prime contractor, was leading the initiative.

Issue The programme was highly complex and started in a haphazard way. This led to confusion, tensions and delays. In particular the programme risk management system that was implemented was overwhelmed with issues, and risks, to add to the confusion. The department heads were so concerned by this that they threatened the prime contractor with a breach of contract for lack of effective risk management processes and practices.

Solution Karena 'parked' the current data and Excel spreadsheets and set up a new system based on ABCD risk management and the Assure web-based tool. The system was implemented 'top-down' so that the programme risks could be highlighted and managed before dropping down into projects and sub-projects. Karena established strict escalation rules so that only risks and issues that were appropriate were escalated to the joint programme risk review board which met on a weekly basis until the programme stabilised, and then on a monthly basis. The web-based tool ensured that senior management could see all relevant risks and what was being done about them, but was not distracted by 'noise'. The programme quickly stabilised and was ultimately hailed as a great success.

> **Learning** It is not always the best solution to just do something rather than nothing. In this situation, the original risk management team had just done what they had always done by implementing simple risk processes and spreadsheets. This would have been fine for the small-scale projects that they had been used in before but in this large-scale and complex programme they added to the risk rather than reducing it. Applying appropriate risk processes and tools to your situation is crucial. Even if you may have to delay implementation to do it right, it's better than creating confusion first and then having to rectify it. Always start top-down to identify the strategic risk first and use strong escalation procedures.

What do the first ten weeks look like?

The answer to this question very much depends on your position regarding a new (or upgraded) risk management process and choice of software support tools. The following suggested plan assumes that you are clear on the preferred process and toolset and is based on wide experience of implementations. However, if you are completely unsure of what your risk management process and toolset will be, you may well take the first ten weeks to decide this. Be careful if this is the case; management expects results so make sure that you manage expectations carefully.

Week 1: Get to know your stakeholders

First impressions will influence the way a relationship will develop in the first few months. Start by understanding the key stakeholders, what their roles are and how each could impact on your success. These will typically include: your boss, work colleagues, your risk management team, functional heads, key opinion leaders, subject matter experts, customers and suppliers.

Do not go into initial meetings or telephone conversations without stopping and thinking things through. What is the impression you want to give, and what do you need to do to make sure you succeed? Think about what could go wrong, and what you can do to make sure risks are avoided or mitigated. Make sure that initial conversations focus on the other person, not you, so take time to really understand what their agenda is, what their concerns are and what their ideas are for the future. Try not to state your ideas at the initial meeting – it is much better just to listen hard. Indeed it is often said that influence most belongs to the person who says least during the meeting but provides the summary at the end and proposes the action plan.

Use this time to assess your stakeholders formally, perhaps using the approach described in Chapter 5. Focus on the stakeholders who have the greatest power or influence over your work, and try to understand the politics of the situation. Think hard about how you can win round any highly influential people who may oppose your ideas, and consider ways of using the support of your advocates to win round other opinion leaders.

Develop a communication plan that includes face-to-face discussions where possible to improve the support for your team from all the highly influential stakeholders. Finally, do not overlook the fact that a key stakeholder may well be the previous incumbent of the job you are starting. If they are still around and available, take time to learn from their knowledge of previous successes and failures.

Critically evaluate each aspect of your risk management team and identify those areas that you consider to be strengths and weaknesses, and areas that reflect opportunities and threats. Make a quick list, but then prioritise it down to the top ones in each category. Recognise that this will reflect your first impressions, so some of your conclusions will be valid whilst others may be incorrect. Take time to validate your thoughts with your boss and other key stakeholders. This will provide an opportunity to get to know them better and to start thinking about ways to address weaknesses and exploit strengths. Here's an example:

Strengths	Weaknesses
CEO is a strong champion of risk management Budget agreed for improvements	No common risk management process across business No consistent risk management tools Poor learning from operational failures
Opportunities	**Threats**
XYZ programme could be a good pilot implementation New regulatory rules could be met by new risk management procedures	Poor quarter figures may reduce available budget for risk management initiatives

Another consistent way of assessing the current state of the business is to undertake a strategic risk assessment using a quick assumption check. This is described in Fast Track top ten, number 2, and will give you a view of the 'as is' state of the business before you consider any change initiative.

Week 2: Decide on your process and tools, and act

It's now time to make final decisions and act. Assuming that you now know your preferred risk management process and toolset, it's time to communicate your decision. You will already have discussed the pros and cons in week 1 so this is making the formal communication to the business. If you have taken all the steps suggested in week 1, it should be no more than a formality.

You now need to train your team in the process and toolset. If the process and tool is familiar, you may wish to do this yourself but, if you are buying in the process and/or tool, it may be more effective to get the vendor to do the training. First-hand training is always better than second-hand training.

If you are training the team, this should ideally be done on your selected toolset. Therefore make sure that your toolset is live and available before the process training. Blended training tends to be the most effective when the process and tool are seen as a seamless system. Get as close to this ideal as you can.

Week 3: Sell the process and tool to the wider business

Senior management should all be sold on your proposed changes by now but the rest of the business need to buy in to a reasonable degree as well. Schedule a series of briefing sessions to cover as much of the business as possible. Arrange for a senior manager to act as a 'champion' to introduce each session and overtly express their support for your initiative. You and your team then need to do focused presentations that cover the following concerns:

→ Where is risk management in the business now?

→ What are the current perceived weaknesses (audience participation is powerful here)?

→ What is the new process and tool (or proposed changes to the current process)?

→ What will be the benefits of the changes?

→ How will this be implemented?

→ What do you want from the audience?

Above all, you have to get the point over that the new process and tool-set will make managers' lives easier. This will arise from identifying risks more effectively, making risk administration easier and actively helping them to manage risks.

QUICK TIP LOOK FOR EVIDENCE
Analyse the facts and opinions of others in order to get to the facts – seek concrete examples. Making decisions on poor information will lead to poor initiatives.

Week 4: Start risk identification

With your team trained and the business briefed, now is the time to go out and capture risk data. Whether you use workshops or interviews to do this will probably depend upon your chosen process but remember to consider the pros and cons of each approach as covered in Fast Track top ten, number 3.

Schedule the sessions to take as little of the interviewee's time as possible. You and your team have budgeted time and resource for this activity; the business, and therefore the interviewees, inevitably won't have.

Your team are freshly trained, so, while their enthusiasm will be high, they are going to take short-cuts and generally make mistakes. They are still learning the process (and tool) but now it is 'on the job'. You must manage this early phase as best you can by being directly involved as much as possible. This is not the time to take a 'hands off' approach. It may even be appropriate for you to lead directly at this stage and for your team members to watch and learn.

Concentrate on quality rather than quantity of data. It's much better that you identify the top five risks accurately rather than capturing 100 risks roughly. The main focus should be on communication, so take a step back after capturing each statement and ask yourself if other people would understand the point of the risk without the need for further explanation. Also, get the balance right between too much and too little information. Too much data will not be read but too little will not convey the essence.

QUICK TIP TRY THE 'TWITTER' TEST
Try to condense your risk statements into the standard Tweet length of 140 characters. This should ensure that they are concise and actually get read.

Week 5: Set up and run the first risk review board

Depending on the size of your enterprise, you may need this week to complete your interviews/workshops but at the very least you need to structure and schedule your first risk review board. The structure and function of the board is described in Fast Track top ten, number 6.

Be under no illusion, the risk review board is the focal point of the risk management process and the first board is where you will be judged. You can manage expectations by limiting the scope of the first board to concentrate on:

→ understanding and agreeing the risks

→ prioritising the risks (e.g. by adding criticality and controllability ratings)

→ agreeing risk owners and risk action managers.

This is a full agenda for a first meeting and getting to an agreed, prioritised risk register with responsibilities allocated are achievable objectives for a first board.

The success of the risk review board will also depend greatly on who attends and, in particular, getting the support of your senior management 'risk champion'. If they cannot attend this first board, then there is a strong case for rescheduling to a time that they can definitely attend. Just their presence will make proceedings much smoother. It's worth noting that this meeting is called a risk review *board* rather than risk meeting as it is meant to encourage senior management to attend.

Use your chosen risk tool carefully in the risk review board. The ideal scenario, if you have a web based tool, is to project the live data on to a screen and update in real time. Paper can be used as a back-up and to give people the means to make notes but try and get people to think about how they will interact with the tool going forward.

Week 6: Coach risk planning

Having agreed a risk register with roles and responsibilities, you may be tempted to think that you now just sit back and wait for risk owners to 'manage' risk action mangers in the production of their risk plans. Well, something might happen if you sit back and wait, but it won't be consistent or efficient.

Risk planning is one of those activities that sounds obvious but isn't. Fast Track top ten, number 5 explains how thinking can be efficiently channelled to make sure that risk plans are effective without going overboard. You and your team need to schedule time with each allocated risk assessment manager to go through their allocated risks and demonstrate best-practice risk planning. This should not take too long and it is probably appropriate to go through one risk plan in detail and then leave the manager to do the rest. Make it clear that it is the responsibility of the risk owner to make sure that the risk action manager completes the risk plan and updates it going forward, but you and your team are always there for any risk action manager questions regarding process.

QUICK TIP REVIEW – PROCESS VS CONTENT
You and your risk team should focus on the risk management process not the content. You will only get people to take responsibility for their risks if you make them responsible for their own risk data content.

It's also now time to take stock of your progress to date. Pay particular attention to your boss, and get to understand them better. What is their preferred leadership style, what are their major opportunities and threats, and how do they feel your first five weeks have progressed?

During this week make sure you get on top of your day-to-day administration and clear as much of your in-box as possible. Ensure that your email list is under control, and take time to delegate non-critical tasks to members of the team as early as possible. Remember that it is much better to deal with issues early, before they become crises.

Week 7: Commence the second round of risk identification

The second round of risk interviews/workshops is similar to the first round but with a couple of big differences.

Firstly, you will be delegating far more responsibility to your team this time around. If the first round has gone reasonably smoothly, the team should be able to step up to the responsibility but keep an eye on individuals and get feedback from the people that they are interacting with. Some people are very good at this role but many don't have the necessary interpersonal skills to deal with people effectively, and particularly on such a touchy subject as 'risk'. Keep this situation under review and accept that you may have to replace team members who do not have these 'soft skills' – you can teach process but it's very difficult to change people's personality.

Secondly, the second round is the first opportunity to cross-communicate risks, or assumptions if you are following an ABCD-based process. Note that this cross-communication is defined and rigorous for ABCD assumptions but can get controversial when sharing risks, as the negative language can get emotive.

In essence each session will cover the following processes:

→ review previously captured risks/assumptions

→ check they are still valid (and wording is still valid)

→ check ratings

→ check the risk plan is moving (but don't get into detail – you don't have the time)

→ capture new risks/assumptions.

Week 8: Set up and run a second risk review board

Again, this is similar to the first risk review board in Week 5, but with two big differences.

Firstly you should now be delegating running of the board to your team members. Depending on how you structure the governance, there may be multiple levels of risk review board (e.g. programme and multiple projects) so the team will have to cover these. Try and support them as much as possible by scheduling boards so that you can attend each one. It is not a good idea to let a team member run a board after just seeing you run one. There is much subtlety in the process that will not be realised in one session.

Secondly, you are now entering the 'ongoing' phase of the risk process. This means that the agenda shifts to:

→ reviewing new risk plans and approving or rejecting them

→ reviewing current risk ratings based on the risk plan status and updating them

→ reviewing new risks and agreeing ratings and allocating roles.

For subsequent risk review boards you only need to review risks that have no risk plans, new risk plans or risk plans that have at least one overdue step. In this way, you focus only on the 'exceptions' and it makes the board focused and quick. Perceptions here are very important and your boss will expect to see momentum building and the process becoming more efficient, so focus on these elements.

Week 9: Reflect and learn

Now stop and review where you are. Take an hour or so at the start of the week to sit back and reflect on what has gone well, and what has gone badly, and why. Go back to your original plan or to-do list and check off the items you have delivered against, and critically review areas where you failed to meet expectations.

Meet with your boss and ask for an informal review of your progress. Many bosses are not very good at doing formal performance reviews, but nevertheless it is an essential part of continuous improvement. Then meet with your other stakeholders and get their inputs into what has gone well, and what they would like to see changed.

And while you are doing this, the third round of the process will have commenced but you should now be in a 'hands off' mode and empowering your team to run the mechanics of the process.

Week 10: Develop your two-year plan

Over the last nine weeks you have built your reputation and credibility as a risk management leader, you have developed important relationships with influential stakeholders, and your confidence has grown. You will by now have an opinion on what you want to achieve based on facts and the advice of experts around the business. Now is the time to develop your two-year plan, and seek to influence the strategic direction of the business.

A lot will depend on whether you are starting from scratch or taking over an existing team, but in either case start by reflecting on your earlier vision and update it if necessary. Perhaps you can be more ambitious in implementing a risk management framework and are now targeting a full enterprise risk management system, or perhaps you want to focus on getting risk management champions up and running in all functional teams. Then work back and identify what needs to be done and achieved on a month-by-month basis. Keep the plan for year two at a high level, but plan the first three months of year one in detail.

Once you have your plan, practise what you preach and identify the key assumptions that you are making and assess these for risk. Identify corrective actions and build these into your plan.

Finally, you should be as specific as possible about how you will know if you are succeeding. Set key performance indicators that you can monitor on a month-to-month basis that will let you and your boss know if you are on track. Make sure that at least one indicator tracks the financial benefits of your work, as this will help you to justify future investment in you and your team.

QUICK TIP IDEAS DATABASE
Set up a simple database of ideas for your team. Start with a simple spreadsheet or whiteboard, classify each idea as to whether it is a major new insight of continuous improvement and make sure that something happens to each idea.

Checklist

What do I need to know?

During your first ten weeks in a new job, start gathering information that will help you to deliver results, build your team and develop your career. Use this list to check that you have the gathered the necessary information and where there is still a bit more or a lot more to be done. Use a simple Red-Amber-Green status where: Red = major gaps in current knowledge and immediate action is required, and Amber = some knowledge is missing and may need to be addressed at some stage in the future.

Obviously your emphasis on this will depend on your situation. If you are changing company or industry, then most of the red issues may be in the top two topics and so on.

TOPIC	INFORMATION	RAG
Business context	The major trends inside and outside the industry that will impact what you do, how you do it and your innovation priorities	
Business strategy	The overall strategy for the business in terms of its products and markets and the basis on which it differentiates itself in the market	
Team objectives	The key performance indicators that will be used to assess whether you and your team have been a success	
Stakeholders	Those individuals or groups that you will work with and that will influence the success or failure of your risk management activities	
The team	Individual members of your risk management team – their names, their backgrounds and their relative strengths and weaknesses	
Roles	Defined risk management roles and responsibilities needed to deliver results – internal to the team or external contributors	
Customers	Your top five internal or external customers and their specific musts and wants	
Suppliers	Your top ten suppliers – who they are and how they contribute to the success of your team	
Your boss	Your operational manager – who they are, their preferred style, and what it is that really makes them tick	
The director	The person leading risk management activities within the business, and possibly the person whose job you aspire to	
Key opinion leaders	People across the organisation whose expert knowledge and opinion is respected by others – who they are and what they each have to offer	

TOPIC	INFORMATION	RAG
Current commitments	The current operational risk management activities – what they are and what it will take to succeed	
Future workload	Future expectations in terms of what needs to be delivered when, and by whom	
Budget	The amount of funding available for your risk management activities – where this will come from and what the sign-off process is	
Resources	The people, facilities, equipment, materials and information available to you for your risk management activities	
Scope	The boundaries that have been set for you and your team – the things you are not allowed to do	
Key events	The major events that are happening within the business that will influence what you need to do and when	
Potential problems	The risks you face going forward – the things that could go wrong based on the assumptions you have made	
SWOT	The relative strengths, weaknesses, opportunities and threats for your risk management team	
Review process	The formal review process for your internal team reviews, and where key performance indicators will be reviewed with your boss	

STOP – THINK – ACT

Now put together a plan for your first ten weeks:

What should I do?	What do I need to achieve?
Who do I need to involve?	Who needs to be involved and why?
What resources will I require?	What information facilities, materials, equipment of budget will be required?
What is the timing?	When will tasks be achieved? Week 1 Week 2 Week 3 Week 4 Week 5 Week 6 Week 7 Week 8 Week 9 Week 10

Visit **www.Fast-Track-Me.com** to use the Fast Track online planning tool.

This expert makes a very academic argument. I find myself torn between thinking that it is either very clever or misses the point. You judge.

Intelligence sources in risk management

Professor Petter Gottschalk Norwegian School of Management

There is a lot to learn from police investigations and intelligence when collecting information for risk management. The police have a number of sources, some of which are certainly applicable to business management as well. In this perspective, it is important for strategic corporate social responsiblity to be aware of the variety of information sources available. I choose to classify information sources into the following categories based on conversations with UK and Norwegian police officials:

1 *Interview*. By means of *interrogation* of witnesses, suspects, reference persons and experts, information is collected on crimes, criminals, times and places, organisations, criminal projects, activities, roles, etc.

2 *Network*. By means of *informants* in the criminal underworld as well as in legal businesses, information is collected on actors, plans, competitors, markets, customers, etc. Informants often have connections with persons that an investigating colleague would not be able to approach formally.

3 *Location*. By analysing potential and actual *crime scenes* and potential criminal scenes, information is collected on criminal procedures, preferences, crime evolution, etc. Hot spots and traces are found. Secret ransacking of suspicious places is part of this information source. Pictures in terms of crime scene photographs are important information elements.

4 *Documents*. Studying documents from *confiscations* may provide information on ownership, transactions, accounts, etc.

5 *Observation*. By means of *anonymous personal presence* both individuals and activities can be observed. Both in the physical and the virtual world, observation is important in financial crime intelligence. An example is digital forensics, where successful cybercrime intelligence requires computer skills and modern systems in policing. Digital forensics is the art and science of applying computer science to aid the legal process. It is more than the technological, systematic inspection of electronic systems and their contents for evidence or supportive evidence of a criminal act. Digital forensics requires specialised expertise and tools when applied to intelligence in important areas such as online victimisation of children.

6 *Action*. For example, *provocation* is an action by the investigating unit to cause reactions that represents intelligence information. In the case of online victimisation of children, online grooming offenders in a paedophile ring are identified and their reaction to provocations leads intelligence officers to new nodes (persons, computers) and new actual and potential victims. While the individual paedophile is mainly concerned with combining indecent image impression and personal fantasy to achieve personal satisfaction, online organisers of sexual abuse of children are doing it for profit. By claiming on the internet to be a boy or girl of nine years of age, police provoke contact with criminal business enterprises making money on paedophile customers. Undercover operations by police officers also belong to the action category of information sources.

7 *Surveillance*. Surveillance of places by means of *video cameras* as well as microphones for viewing and listening belong to this information source. Many business organisations have surveillance cameras on their premises to control entrances and other critical areas. It is possible for the police to be listening in on what is discussed in a room without the participants knowing. For example, police in a country identified which room was used by local Hells Angels members for crime planning and installed listening devices in that room.

8 *Communication control.* Wire tapping in terms of *interception* belongs to this information source. Police are listening in on what is discussed on a telephone or data line without the participants knowing. In the UK, the interception of communications (telephone calls, emails, letters, etc.), whilst generating intelligence to identify more conventional evidential opportunities, is excluded from trial evidence by law, to the evident incredulity of foreign law enforcement colleagues.

9 *Physical material.* Investigation of material to identify, for example, *fingerprints* on doors or bags, or material to identify blood type from blood splatters. Another example is legal visitation, which is an approach to identify illegal material. DNA is emerging as an important information source, where DNA is derived from physical material such as hair or saliva from a person. Police search is one approach to physical material collection.

10 *Internet.* As an *open source*, the internet is as important to corporate crime intelligence for general information and specific events as it is to everyone else.

11 *Policing systems.* Readily available in most police agencies are *police records*. For example, DNA records may prove helpful when obtaining DNA material from new suspects. Similarly, corporate social responsibility units may develop records that do not violate privacy rights.

12 *Employees.* Information from the *local community* is often supplied as tips to local police, using law enforcement tip lines. Similarly, a corporate social responsibility unit is receiving tips from employees in various departments.

13 *Accusations.* Victimised persons and goods file a *claim* with the corporate investigation unit or the unit for corporate social responsibility.

14 *Exchange.* International *policing cooperation* includes exchange of intelligence information. International partners for national police include national police in other countries as well as multinational organisations such as Europol and Interpol.

Similarly, trade organisations and other entities for business organisations create exchanges for financial crime intelligence.

15 *Media*. By reading newspapers and watching TV, intelligence officers get access to *news*.

16 *Control authorities*. Cartel agencies, stock exchanges, tax authorities and other control authorities are *suppliers of information* to the corporate executives in case of suspicious transactions.

17 *External data storage*. A number of business and government organisations store information that may be useful in financial crime intelligence. For example, telecom firms store data about traffic, where both sender and receiver are registered with date and time of communication.

Not all of these information sources are recommended for a fast track to success. The list is supplied to encourage your own imagination when faced with misconduct in your own organisation.

EXPERT VOICE

7

LEADING THE TEAM

Leadership is as important to success as gaining expert knowledge and being familiar with appropriate tools and techniques. Focus on your personal attributes as a manager, and reflect on what it takes to lead and develop a team.

Changing myself

How should I think?

The starting point is to look closely at yourself and reflect on your self-perception. If you are a newly promoted manager make sure you review that self-perception and adjust your way of thinking where necessary. As you get into more challenging jobs, you must move onwards and upwards in your thinking.

All roles are different by nature, but the jump from one grade to the next is probably the most pronounced when you first step into management. How often do we hear people reflecting on how the ace sales representative does not necessarily make the best sales manager? This can be the same for any specialisation. You may have been great at risk management, but can you get others to think and act in same way, and can you lead and motivate a team of people that may not even report to you?

You need to start thinking as a risk management professional. Whilst it may be the most enjoyable job you will ever do, it is not something you do for the fun of it – you've got to make or save money. We define risk management as the proactive avoidance of risks and exploitation of opportunities and, therefore, as a manager in this area you must drive results to the bottom line.

You will also need to be more aware of the whole organisation, and be proactive in terms of anticipating change. How much time do you spend thinking about future risk areas; is it really enough; do they change all the time? One of the key attributes of the FastTrack manager is that they will spend more time looking at what is happening in other functions or businesses.

Think differently; think risk and opportunity.

QUICK TIP YOUR NEXT JOB
Think about your next career step and imagine how different it will be, then list the things you can do today to help prepare for this next challenge.

What personal attributes will I need?

The starting point for managing an effective team is to manage yourself. Whenever I see a manager setting career and personal development activities for members of their team I'm often impressed by their professionalism. Unfortunately, all too often they have not been so diligent with their own personal development planning.

Conducting a self-assessment against four dimensions – knowledge, competencies, attitudes and behaviours – is a useful starting point. Do you have the necessary knowledge about best practice risk management processes and tools? Are you able to think creatively, conduct analyses to understand why things happen (or could happen), review risk management processes and put into place plans that will deliver benefits on time and within budget? Do you have the right attitude in terms of being positive, seeking synergies between other people's ideas and constantly looking for new thinking on risk management? And do you actively support others in the risk management process, and have the determination to overcome obstacles?

Use a structured approach to identify specific areas in each of the four categories – knowledge, competencies, attitudes and behaviours – that you need to work on. However, before taking action, take time to discuss your thoughts with your boss or your coach and seek evidence of good or poor performance. Perhaps summarise your thoughts in the form of a SWOT (strengths, weaknesses, opportunities and threats) analysis before putting a plan together. However, do not be overambitious and try and develop yourself too quickly – becoming an effective risk manager takes time.

> **QUICK TIP BUSINESS STRATEGY**
> Make sure you know what the strategy of your business is, and focus your risk management activities on the specific imperatives for the next one to three years, both in terms of risk management saving money and making money.

What leadership style is appropriate?

These may be your first tentative steps into management or you may be an experienced manager, but in either case take time to reflect on what leadership style may be appropriate for your new role. One way of thinking about this is to consider the extent to which you involve others in events and key decisions. One extreme is to be dictatorial and adopt a 'command' style where you make the decisions in isolation without involving or consulting others. For example, you may decide what the priority ideas are and simply tell people to get on with implementing them. At the other extreme you allow the group to decide what ideas to choose through a consensus driven approach. There are, of course, stages between the two. You may choose to ask questions of key managers in order to confirm facts such as the threat from the competition, or you may consult them individually or as a group and ask their opinion – but then still make the decisions yourself. This model of leadership is effectively a continuum from command at the top to consensus at the bottom – see the figure overleaf.

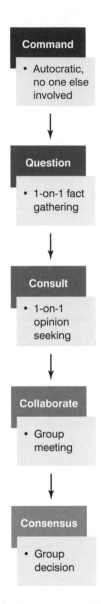

So, is there a preferred style for your role? The reality is that there is no one right or wrong answer, and that your choice will vary depending on the situation. Fast Track managers assess each situation quickly and are then flexible enough to adapt their style based on three criteria.

The first is **time**. Involving others (moving from the top to the bottom on the continuum) increases both the time delay in the decision and the number of people and time involved in the decision-making process. This can cause serious delays where choices need to be made quickly.

The second is **commitment**. So long as the team members respect their manager and the more involved people feel the more likely they are to commit to decisions and actively support the implementation of new ideas. The third dimension is **quality**. There is no point making decisions in isolation if you lack the facts or experience: you will simply be risking the failure of the idea and exposing your reputation. At the same time, if you are to allow the team to make the final go/no-go on decisions and to set priorities, you need to make sure that whatever it comes out with will be acceptable to the business. These three elements are represented in the figure below. Be clear about the boundaries regarding timings, outcomes and limitations in terms of what would and would not be an acceptable solution – they can be as tight or loose as is appropriate, but once set you will find them very difficult to change. People get used to a manager's style and adapt their behaviour to conform, or move out if they don't like it. Once they have experience of your style, they may well be uncomfortable if you try to change it. Of course, you will change your style according to the situation and they will appreciate that and why you are doing it. You can't use a collaborative style when there's a fire in the factory and you're in charge, but it may be most appropriate to spend a lot of time with the team discussing how to put things back to normal when the fire is out.

Time invested and speed — **Commitment** to decision

Quality

Reflect on your style of leadership using the simple list below. What is your preferred style? When would a consensus style be more appropriate and when would a command style be more effective? Whilst everyone has a preferred style, Fast Track managers are comfortable operating at all points on the continuum, but to do this they will have developed appropriate skills.

→ **Command**: ability to analyse the situation, solve problems alone, make decisions, proactively think ahead and manage risks, and the willingness and ability to tell others what to do.

→ **Question**: ability to ask open and closed questions and, most importantly, listen to the answers without interrupting to the point where you have sufficient facts to make the decision.

→ **Consult**: willingness and ability to listen hard to what others are telling you. Listen to subtler signals such as feelings and opinions, and ability to seek proposals from others and integrate into decisions.

→ **Collaborate**: ability to manage meetings effectively with clear objectives, agenda, and logistics. Willingness to challenge the group, discuss ways forward and manage conflict where there are differences of opinion.

→ **Consensus**: ability to set the group boundaries for the joint session, facilitate discussion, build consensus in a team and gain commitment to outputs. Remember that not everyone needs to agree with the decision of the group, but they do all need to commit to it.

Coaching

Whilst not part of the formal leadership model above, coaching should play a role in developing yourself as well as members of your team. It is said that if you want to master a particular discipline, then teach it. Fast Track managers develop excellent coaching skills and are in turn prepared to be coached – helping individuals develop core skills or resolve barriers.

Motivating the individual

How do I get the most out of each member of my team?

Whether people across the business report to you, or are simply contributors to your risk management activities, think carefully about how you will keep them motivated and how to maximise their contribution to the current risk management process and future developments. First focus on the **behaviour** you are looking for. It may be that you want people to follow the processes rigorously or you may want them to use their own initiative on which ones they need to implement. Whatever it is, people's behaviour will be determined by what comes before they need to do the task, called **antecedents**, and what comes afterwards, the **consequences** – see the figure below.

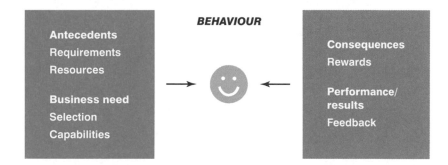

> → **Antecedents**. Once you are sure you have chosen the right people for the task, set them up for success by making it clear what is expected of them and what the outcomes should look like. Targets should be stretching but should not over-stretch individuals, as this can be demotivating. They should reflect the business needs you are looking to address whether these relate to the development of a new product or finding a creative way to open up a new market. Check that individuals have the necessary skills, knowledge and experience, and arrange personal development activities for those that need it. Finally think about the resources they will need to be effective. These may include time, facilities, materials, equipment, information and budget.

> → **Consequences**. Look closely at each task and assess the natural consequences for each person. If they do a great job, what happens to them or what benefits do they receive? Avoid situations where there are positive consequences for doing a bad job. For example, if someone fails to implement a new idea effectively because they are keen to move on to a different project, find a way of ensuring this does not happen unless they buckle down to the implementation. Conversely, think of ways to use consequences as a way of driving positive

behaviour. For example, if someone arrives late for the start of a risk workshop, ask them to capture the discussion on the flip chart or to take the notes. The most effective ways of keeping people motivated is typically through the use of natural (non-financial) rewards, such as providing opportunities for personal development, allowing people to present to senior managers, seeing an idea through to completion or simply taking the time to stop and say 'Thank you'.

For example, think about the next risk review board you will be running, and use the model to check that you are set up for success. What do you need to put in place in terms of **antecedents**, and what do you need to do to ensure that the **consequences** of participating are positive?

FACILITATING A RISK REVIEW BOARD

Antecedents	→ Put together an invitation that clearly explains the objectives of the meeting, the roles and responsibilities, and an agenda with timing (allow enough time).
	→ Invite the right people (e.g. the risk owners and the risk champion) in order to get the right engagement and decision making to deal with the risks that will be discussed.
	→ Ask a member of your team to ensure that all relevant discussions are captured.
	→ Ask a member of the team to drive the risk management tool to maintain real-time engagement as appropriate.
	→ Ensure the room you have is large enough, has plenty of natural light and has the appropriate layout.
	→ Send an email reminder out a few days beforehand asking all participants to clear their diaries.
	→ Think about the risks to the meeting: what could go wrong? Plan mitigating actions.
Behaviour	→ The team ensures that the risks are discussed in a focused way and that the members of the team capture risk plans and update them efficiently.
	→ The participants remain focused, avoiding spurious or unnecessary discussions.
	→ The participants feedback their appreciation of the value of the workshop.
Consequences	→ Allow the team to engage with the (senior) risk owners at appropriate points in the meeting.
	→ Ensure that junior team members get due credit for their efforts.
	→ Allocate a budget for a team dinner as a way of encouraging future participation and celebrating success.

Create the right environment

Why is this important?

Risk is an emotive subject that can be difficult to discuss freely. You and your team must create an environment where risk can be discussed freely and positively, or the whole risk management process will become a struggle that will be demotivating for all concerned.

What culture is best?

There is no one right answer to this and it will vary depending on your preferred style and the business context or situation at a point in time. However, there are basic components that tend to result in an environment that will be more conducive to effective risk management:

→ **Risk identification is good.** Create an environment where it is a positive attribute to identify risks. This is extremely important as the potential negativity of the content can encourage participants to be 'quiet' at best and even dishonest if they feel threatened. For example, one departmental head made a clear statement at the start of one risk review board that no one would ever get 'into trouble' for raising risks, but they would get into serious trouble if risks impacted that were not raised and should have been. This encouraged stakeholders to think harder and even realise that it was best to get their risks on the table so that the value of their role in managing them could be fully appreciated.

→ **Blame-free.** Following on from this, there needs to be a culture that 'we are all in this together'. Even when there is obviously one party causing the risk, you need to avoid pointing the finger and just get on with the process of prioritisation and risk planning. Both the risk team and stakeholders can and should get enormous credit for risk management.

→ **Learning organisation.** Risk management should be about proactively managing risk but it should also encompass ways of learning from previous risks that were not managed. Find some way of formalising the lessons learned and reinforcing the importance of doing so.

Building the team

What makes a great team?

So, you have a great leadership style that is flexible enough to cope with different situations, and you have a number of highly motivated and skilled people to work with, but that does not necessarily make them a great team. So, what do the successful risk management teams do that differentiates them from average performers? Read through the following checklist, and reflect on what you need to do as leader of the team in order to ensure success.

→ The team will have great clarity in its goals and have a real sense of shared purpose. Fast Track teams will have such clarity of vision that they will know how they want to be remembered long after they have been disbanded.

→ The team will have a strong and enthusiastic leader who provides direction, is supportive of team members and willing to shoulder responsibility when things do not go according to plan. They are often not the expert or specialist, but they understand how to bring experts together and get them to perform effectively as a unit. Members will be empowered to take action, and be willing to take on the leadership role themselves as and when required.

→ Fast Track teams also accept that things will change, and have an ability to accept this and be flexible in order to bring things back on track. Perhaps a team is implementing a major change programme, and within the first week a key member of the team leaves. The team will reappraise the situation quickly but calmly, explore creative options for dealing with the situation and move on.

→ They will have shared values and a common set of operating principles. A team of people with a variety of skills and experiences needs to be unified by common beliefs. We see the enormous power that the adoption of a common set of religious beliefs can have (both positive and negative), and whilst levels of fanaticism are rarely positive, shared values will often provide the team with enormous energy and commitment.

→ Ideally, the shared values then extend into a general respect and liking for each other where members of the team trust each other and genuinely have fun working together. The Armed Forces will always ensure that their teams spend time gaining shared experiences together in a safe environment, before they are asked to put their lives on the line.

→ There will be issues to deal with, but the Fast Track teams will manage these quickly and sensitively before they become crises. To do this they need to have open and honest communication, and work in a blame-free environment where rewards for success are shared.

→ Whilst these teams will focus on their primary objectives, they will have a feeling of shared responsibility and be supportive of each other. They will take time out to continuously learn and develop new skills – both individually and as a team. This necessitates keeping an eye on how they are performing, and scanning other similar teams in order to identify alternative approaches that could be adopted.

→ Finally, the team will be balanced in terms of the skills and capabilities of team members, and in terms of the roles they each fulfil. They have people capable of creative challenge, but they also need people willing to get their heads down in order to put the work in and deliver the results. You may want to allocate them roles reflecting different ways of thinking as reflected in Edward de Bono's 'six hats' – see the figure below.[1] You may not wish to allocate these roles, but reflecting on which of your team members operate naturally in one of these hats will help you to make the most of your people and plug potential gaps.

• White	Focus on evidence and the facts
• Red	Focus on emotion and gut feel
• Yellow	Focus on the positive – why it will work
• Green	Focus on lateral thinking and brainstorming
• Black	Focus on the negative – devil's advocate
• Blue	Focus on evaluation – pros and cons

[1] de Bono, Edward (1986) *Six Thinking Hats*, Harmondsworth: Viking.

How should I develop the team?

As well as developing the skills of individual members of your team, you need to build them into a team. Review the list of attributes of a great team above, and make a note of any area where you feel there is a need for improvement.

Next, assess where you think the team is now in terms of their stage of development. This is particularly important for those working in the area of risk management, as team members are often part-time. Each team will go through various stages of development, and your role as the leader will be to recognise where they are, and to take action to move them to a state where they are their most productive. Consider the model shown below[2]:

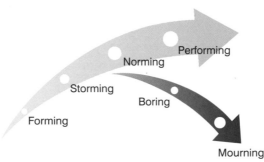

STAGE	DESCRIPTION	LEADERSHIP ACTIONS
Forming	The team is brought together for the first time, and needs to spend time understanding each other and what they are each contributing.	Think carefully about whom to involve in each team and make sure there is a balance in terms of different roles, skills and experience. Allow people to get to know each other personally, and set simple tasks to allow people to work together for the first time and get a quick win.
Storming	Initially they will each be keen to contribute, and will want to have their say in terms of who fulfils which role and who will have the greatest sway over the outcomes. If this is not managed carefully, teams can become very 'political', where individuals jockey for power and positions. This can result in a downward spiral in terms of effectiveness.	Make sure that the early tasks the team undertakes are straightforward and will result in success. Establish team roles and communicate them clearly so that everyone knows what their and other people's contribution is. There will always be the potential for conflict, so look for it, and seek consensus on key decisions at an early stage.

[2] Concept developed by Bruce Wayne Tuckman in the short article 'Developmental sequence in small groups', 1965, *Psychology Bulletin*, 63(6), pp. 384–99 (Naval Medical Research Institute, Bethesda, MD).

STAGE	DESCRIPTION	LEADERSHIP ACTIONS
Norming	As the team settles down, it needs to adopt norms in terms of how members work together. This needs to cover decision making, communication and meeting disciplines. Without common processes a lot of the energy and enthusiasm of the team can be dissipated.	Be clear about what will happen at each meeting, and that there are agreed objectives, an agenda with timings and appropriate resources. Communicate your leadership style in terms of the circumstances in which you will seek the team's views.
Performing	The team should now have clear roles and be working effectively as a unit. This is where results are produced, and you need to keep the team in this positive and effective mode.	Monitor performance regularly, and take swift action to resolve issues before they become crises. Spend one-on-one time with each member of the team to keep them motivated.
Boring	For teams that have been together for a long time, there is a danger that they stop challenging the way they work. This is common on major projects where individuals can easily become complacent with their roles and get into a rut. If left unnoticed, it can result in the team getting bored, and performance can quickly fall off.	Find ways of constantly challenging the team as a whole and as individuals. Consider bringing in new members, or rotate jobs and roles. Perhaps, there will come a point where you need to fundamentally adjust the team's objectives in order to get them to stop and re-evaluate what they are doing.
Mourning	Finally, for high-performing teams, there is always a major sense of loss when a valued member moves on. Even if their replacement appears to have the right profile, there can be resistance, and the team effectively moves back into the 'forming' stage.	When people leave the team, for good or bad reasons, think carefully about the transition. Focus on some of the softer people issues within the team – not simply on updating the plan.

How do I overcome barriers to change?

Implementing any new process, like risk management, is all about change. Recognise that the ideas you and your team generate may be worthwhile, but accept that there will be resistance simply because some people do not like change. The denial, resistance, exploration, commitment (DREC) change model can help to understand the process that people need to go through, and give insights in terms of what you will need to consider when planning changes – see the figure overleaf.

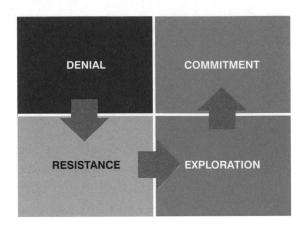

→ **Denial**. People believe that the current situation is perfectly acceptable and refuse to accept that the change is needed or that change will happen. You hear the cry of 'It will never happen' coming from different teams. Most organisations regularly fail to implement changes effectively, and the organisation reverts back to its former state quite quickly. It is perhaps no wonder that people are often cynical and will wait to see if anything actually happens. As the leader of the change, your reputation is on the line. To be taken seriously you have to drive the change through. Accept that some people will be in denial, but find a way of helping them to come to terms with the fact that the change will happen.

→ **Resistance**. Even when people have accepted that the change will happen, many will still be resistant. It is their way of telling you that they are still not convinced that this is the right way to go. Work out counter-arguments in advance, take time to explain the business case for the change, and make it clear why the current situation will not endure, using an example, perhaps of a catastrophic effect of failing to identify and deal with a risk. Identify those people in the business who have bought in to the idea and who are also widely respected. We call these people the key opinion leaders. Use these people to spread the word and explain to others why this change is so vital for the future.

→ **Exploration**. Once there is an acceptance that the change will happen and that it is a good thing, allow people to investigate ways in which it will impact them and their teams for the better, and ways in which they can help with implementation. Get them involved, allow them to ask questions and make sure they are taking action.

→ **Commitment**. Finally, as they start to realise the benefits, take time to capture the early victories, write them up and communicate them across other teams. Often, those that showed the greatest level of resistance, once converted, become your best advocates.

The DREC cycle is a useful way of understanding the natural stages we all go through when faced with change. Some of us will move through the cycle much faster than others, so take time early on to help those that are struggling to move through the cycle.

QUICK TIP CONVERTING SCEPTICS
Very often the people who are most resistant to your proposals will be your strongest supporters when the benefits from risk management start to become evident.

CASE STORY DEFENCE PROJECT, DAVID'S STORY

Narrator David was the risk manager for a large defence project.

Context The customer was paranoid about risk management and insisted that the supplier employed an independent risk management consultancy to 'do' the risk management process.

Issue The independent risk management consultancy was motivated to use the largest team possible to do all of the work in identifying, analysing and even managing the risks on behalf of the supplier and customer teams. This encouraged the project managers and their team to delegate not just the risk process but to assume that they could 'wash their hands' of risk management because someone else was doing it for them. Risk management was consequently very costly and very ineffective as the risk management consultants did not understand the detail of the risks or have the authority or insight to deal with them.

Solution The risk consultancy role was reduced to focus on process only while the responsibility for risk management was set clearly with the project teams. This made the process far more effective and also saved a considerable amount of money.

Learning Risk managers cannot manage risk. The job of a risk manager is to concentrate on the integrity of the risk *process*. The individuals on the project need to focus on the *content*, i.e. to own the risks and manage them.

STOP – THINK – ACT
Reflect on how well you are leading the team and look for ways you could improve. Now think about how well the team is operating and where the team is in the forming to mourning model. What groups affected by the change are not in the 'committed' section of the DREC model?

What should we do?	What actions do we need to take to build the team?
Who do we need to involve?	Who needs to be involved and why?
What resources will we require?	What level of investment would be required?
What is the timing?	What deadlines do we need to meet?

Visit **www.Fast-Track-Me.com** to use the FastTrack online planning tool.

Parametric cost analysis improves the quality of stop–go decisions in pharmaceutical R&D

Professor Giampiero Favato Kingston Business School, London

Pharmaceutical development is a complex, risky and time-consuming process. In a substantial majority of cases, pharmaceutical companies abandon research on new drugs that have undergone clinical testing but have not received marketing approval. Both the extent to which, and the speed at which, the development process makes new therapies available to the public are important measures of the viability of that process. The probability of a new molecular entity in development reaching the market increases with each successive phase of the R&D process. It is estimated that 60 per cent of the active substances currently in discovery will not progress to the more advanced stages of development. These high attrition rates are a major challenge for the industry in the face of demands for increased productivity of new and innovative molecules.

Major pharmaceutical companies are placing significant emphasis on the drive to reduce spiralling R&D expenditure and improve productivity. The optimisation of stop–go decisions is a strategy aimed at a direct and immediate reduction in expenditure. Knowledge of the principles of stop–go decision points within the R&D process is, therefore, of prime importance. By making a careful last-minute decision on a development candidate just before it enters clinical development, a company can reduce considerable wasted effort and resources on those projects with lower anticipated chances of viability, and so maximise the numbers of candidates that complete clinical trials and subsequently prove successful.

The approach to financial evaluation of drug development has been progressively rationalised in parallel with the development of financial and risk analysis quantitative models. Looking at the evolution of R&D risk-adjusted models, financial evaluation has progressively moved away from deterministic quantitative analysis in favour of non-linear, stochastic algorithms. Great emphasis has been placed on the determination of streams of future cash flows, adjusting the present value for time and risk with probability functions, while little attention has been paid to the second driver of value: the cost of clinical trials. A major and contentious issue is whether the cost of a clinical trial can be determined *a priori* with a sufficient degree of statistical confidence.

Parametric cost analysis establishes a clear linkage between cost and a product's technical non-cost parameters by using equations to map measurable system attributes on to cost. The measures of the system attributes are called 'metrics'. The equations are called 'cost estimating relationships' and are obtained by the analysis of cost and technical metric data of products that are analogous to those to be estimated. Today, parametric estimating is typically applied to large systems, such as those found in the US Department of Defense or NASA Research Center. Parametric estimating relies on simulation models that are systems of statistically and logically supported mathematical equations that define the impact of a product's physical, performance and programmatic attributes on cost and schedule. Parameters are tailored to describe the object being estimated and the output of the model is validated with data from past projects. The object to be estimated is described by choosing specific values for the independent variables in the equation that represents the characteristics of the object. The equations are then used to extrapolate from past and current experience to forecast the cost of future products.

The fundamental assumption in parametric cost analysis is that a measurable relationship exists between system attributes and the cost of the system: if a function exists, the attributes are cost drivers. Sample-size variables are constraints on the clinical development process; from optimisation theory it is known that any active constraint generates cost by not permitting full optimisation of the objective and sample-size variables are cost drivers.

The application of parametric estimating methods to the pharmaceutical development process allows the estimation of the direct costs of clinical trials from a derived linear relationship. The derived CER correlates the effect size (in other words the standardised minimal significant outcome, which is a known *a priori* independent variable) to the minimal sample size required to confer statistical significance upon the outcome (independent variable). The parametric methodological perspective actually looks at the sample-size theory as a linear relationship to pre-determine the cost of research. The possibility of estimating the cost of late stage clinical development with an elevated degree of confidence would definitely improve the quality of stop–go decisions and portfolio evaluation in pharmaceutical R&D.

GETTING TO THE TOP

Finally, think about what you need to do to stand out amongst your peers, stay current and then to get ahead. As you progress up the corporate ladder you need to focus continuously on performance, and increasingly look up and out as opposed to in and down. Your personal network will be more and more important, and you will need to start to think and act like a director.

Risk management may be your primary role or it may be an area that you focus on to ensure that business objectives are met. If you want to reach the top in risk management, your aim should probably be to become a chief risk officer (CRO). The CRO role is a fairly recent move by organisations to give risk a higher profile and place it on an equivalent status to finance and IT, for example. Perhaps your organisation does not have a board level CRO role at this time. But perhaps you could be your company's first CRO.

Focus on performance

Fast Track managers know what is important and what is not, and focus on the key performance indicators (KPIs) that have the greatest impact on what they are trying to achieve. At all times they will understand where they are now, what the bottlenecks are and how to clear them. They regularly take time to look around for best practice, to reflect on the past in order to learn from what went well or what could be improved on, and to think ahead to the future so that concerns can be resolved before they become crises. By always delivering, or exceeding, against expectations, they stand out from the pack and will be automatic considerations for promotion at the appropriate time.

Performance snapshot: past – historic

There is a universal complaint from historians that politicians don't learn from the lessons of history. This tends to be true of businesses as well. Without a clear understanding of what has happened before, we risk repeating mistakes from the past, or reacting to a crisis that doesn't actually exist: fixing what's not broke. There was an engineering company, for example, with a poor record for delivering on time and within budget. Its poor past performance may have been undesirable, but the complete lack of competition meant that it was not in crisis; it could improve performance over time without the extra costs involved in treating the situation as a crisis. It could survive with a blasé attitude to risk because if something went wrong, its customers had to wait while things were sorted out. You can imagine the change that it had to go through when competition finally arrived. The company went from learning from past mistakes being voluntary to learning from past mistakes being crucial.

Many organisations maintain a lessons learned database but then rarely use it. The trouble is that they are easy to set up, but difficult to allow easy access to the people who you want to see them. After all, such a database is an important, but commercially sensitive, asset. Think about how you, in your situation, will find out about what has happened before.

For example, during one risk management training session in a large manufacturing company, the participants were asked how they ensured they learned from previous mistakes. They stated that it took them two days to identify databases that may contain useful information, another two days to get security clearance to look at the data, and even then the data was unstructured and virtually useless. Once the manager had left the room, they all admitted that they just didn't bother anymore and started with a blank piece of paper.

Performance snapshot: present – current situation (gap)

The organisation's champions have to focus on the right priorities. If they don't, then they risk turning a problem into a crisis. They will want to know:

→ what is currently going on

→ whether or not they are on track

→ if not, what are the issues and who is dealing with them?

They want this information in a specific way, not as a series of vague intentions. They might use the SMART acronym by saying they want information on projects that is specific, measurable, accurate, relevant and timely.

Performance snapshot: future – predictive

KPIs tend to focus on what has happened historically (just as a profit and loss account will tell you how the business performed in the last reporting period). Check that your risk management KPIs are looking in all three directions – current and future as well as past. However, you need always to see risk management in the context of your business strategy. For example, a phone company undertook many development projects within a year in order to exploit new technologies and to stay ahead of the competition. When asked whether they were concerned about failed projects, the CEO answered that he expected at least 50 per cent of projects to fail, on the basis that if they did not they were probably not being innovative enough as an organisation. He then said that a key skill of their project managers was looking after the team, helping highly skilled people to come to terms with the fact that a project they had invested up to 18 months of their lives in was 'killed off'. In this case, improved risk management would not necessarily benefit the company strategy in the normal sense.

Invite challenge

Who can we get to challenge us?

Fast Track managers never rest on their laurels. You may think that your performance is on track, but as the external business environment changes you need to adapt. Look for ways to introduce challenge to you and your team on a regular basis, aiming to bring in ideas, tools and techniques from recognised risk leaders. Review the different groups:

→ **Other internal teams**. What ideas do they have on risk management?

→ **Customers**. How are their must-haves, needs and wants changing? What future risks might occur as you help to meet those changing requirements? Could you learn from how they deal with risk management?

→ **Competitors**. How well does your business manage risk relative to your main competitors? What are they doing now that could be copied ('swiped' or reverse engineered)?

→ **Supply chain**. What possibilities are there for improved effectiveness and efficiency in the wider operations of the business? What are the risks to you in each link of the chain?

→ **Partners**. What can we learn from them? What opportunities are there for collaboration?

→ **Industry advisers**. What are the experts recommending? What breakthrough tools and techniques have they developed? Search the internet regularly.

These groups are represented in the diagram opposite.

Engage in challenging acts on a regular basis even if you don't need to in order to meet your KPIs because you want to stay ahead of the game. If you are finding it easy to meet the targets set for you, then don't wait for your boss to make them more stretching: do it yourself. Perhaps take time to get involved in areas where you are not confident in order to develop yourself continuously.

Remember to use relevant opportunities for self-development both inside and outside work, within your function and without. Consider the following actions:

→ Get involved in public speaking, such as working on internal management development courses.

→ Commission external studies, such as using undergraduate students.

→ Get involved in an outside body involved with strategic issues relating to risk management.

→ Get on the steering committee for a professional risk management institute.

→ Respond to public enquires (from the government) and try to get on review bodies by developing a reputation.

→ Get experience of board work through acting in the role in a company spin-out or increase your exposure to your own company board and its way of thinking by making presentations when the opportunity arises.

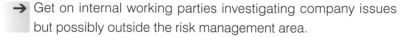

→ Get on internal working parties investigating company issues but possibly outside the risk management area.

Generally engage in what is often termed 'firm building', i.e. building the reputation of your company by focusing on initiatives that are over and above your operational responsibilities. Nothing gets you noticed more than meeting/exceeding your targets *and* firm building at the same time.

How do I keep up to date?

As well as working with other groups inside and outside of the business, think carefully about what additional sources of knowledge and insight you want to receive and how often. There is a wealth of information available from a variety of sources, so you need to be selective as the time you have available for reading is limited and the quality can be variable.

→ **The Web**: provides freely available information from a very wide variety of sources, but is typically unstructured and will contain bias. *Fast Track recommendation*: bookmark and review the websites of your 'top ten' customers and competitors twice a year, and identify up to five other useful websites that provide challenge. Also follow 'social media' sites such as LinkedIn and Twitter. The latter in particular is becoming the fastest way of keeping in touch with the latest developments, and search features can make searches and maintenance relatively easy.

→ **Journals or trade magazines**: available via a subscription and will make the latest ideas and thinking available but will often contain a lot of commercial advertorials. *Fast Track recommendation*: subscribe to the one journal of greatest relevance to you and your main customers/industry for one year and review its value. Once you have read it, make sure you circulate it to other members of your team.

→ **Conferences and exhibitions**: provide a useful opportunity to listen to stimulating presentations and are typically an excellent way of networking with others outside the business, but can be time-consuming and expensive. *Fast Track recommendation*: identify the one conference of greatest relevance to your industry and attend it for two consecutive years. Aim to identify at least three people (other attendees or presenters) to follow up with about specific issues you have. Conferences are much more productive, particularly from a personal marketing perspective, if you are presenting as well as listening.

→ **Communities of practice**: online discussion forums between like-minded people within the innovation community. *Fast Track recommendation*: these can be extremely useful or a complete waste of time, so give it a go and see what value you get. You may also want to consider forming your own but recognise that you will need to put in the necessary time and effort to get it off the ground.

→ **Benchmarking**: perhaps the most valuable way of identifying new ideas and stretching the way you think, but take a certain amount of effort to set up and manage. *Fast Track recommendation*: definitely worth doing if practical, so identify two or three other organisations who you respect from a risk management perspective, and meet them up to four times a year, making sure you use a facilitator and follow a structure agenda to maximise the cross-company learning. Remember that you will have to give value to them as well as the other way round.

→ **Professional bodies**: membership of these bodies becomes more important the more senior you become, and are often a source of free advice. *Fast Track recommendation*: once you have been in your role for at least a year, sign up for an initial trial period and see what benefits you receive.

→ **Fast-Track-Me.com:** all of the key ideas, tools and techniques contained in the complete Fast Track series are available via the internet at **www.Fast-Track-Me.com**. *Fast Track recommendation*: allocate 30 minutes to visit and explore the site. It contains a rich source of tips, tools and techniques, stories, expert voices, and online audits from all of the Fast Track series.

Remember that whatever your source of information, to maximise the benefits you need to put time aside and make the necessary effort.

However, also recognise that you will never have perfect knowledge. Take time to develop your skills in assessing the validity and reliability of the information you have, then decide what level of certainty will be good enough and act on it. Remember as the diagram below shows, seeking information and removing uncertainties becomes more expensive until, for example, the last few per cent is prohibitively expensive. The dangerous area in the middle highlights the risk of making important decisions on limited information.

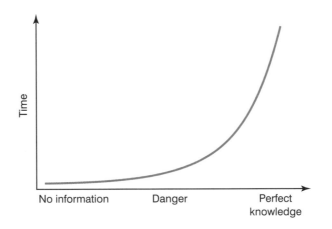

Getting promoted

At the appropriate time the Fast Track manager will seek promotion again. This may occur within a few months or possibly a number of years, but in either case take time to reflect on your state of readiness. Identify the future role you are keen to fulfil, clarify the criteria you will need to satisfy in terms of skills, experience, attitudes and behaviours, and consider how you will visibly demonstrate these attributes to others. Ask yourself, in relation to the following:

→ **Capability**. Do I have what it takes in terms of what I have achieved and learned so far?

→ **Credibility**. Can I convince others that I can and will perform the role well?

→ **Desire**. Do I want the role, and do I have sufficient drive and enthusiasm to do a great job?

→ **Relationships**. Do I have positive working relationships with the right people?

→ **Competitiveness**. Am I the most appropriate candidate, given the internal and external alternatives?

If you have concerns, then put a plan in place to address them. Timing will be key so make sure you are well prepared before putting yourself forward for the role. Learn how to package yourself by seeking advice and gaining feedback.

 CASE STORY MACHINERY MANUFACTURER, MARIEKE'S STORY

Narrator Marieke was a fast-rising manager in a machinery manufacturing company.

Context The company, a successful manufacturer of machinery for the food processing industry, had grown rapidly in a market that was mature but still comprised a large number of inefficient smaller producers. The company's success came as a direct result of sales of an advanced computer-driven processing machine that would dramatically reduce wastage in its customers' operations.

Issue In early 2005, Marieke remembers a meeting with the production team where intensive debate centred around the fact that the company's products were very good but that it could not deliver to specification on time and within budget. Whilst it had a great forward order book and a good relationship with key customers, this clearly represented a significant risk to future success. Sooner or later, Marieke recognised that competition from Italy and Germany would start to take its market share.

Solution Over the previous five years it had become a truly innovative company, but had not focused on operational improvements. Fortunately, during further discussions with the top team, Marieke identified several people who had previously worked with organisations that had adopted 'lean' manufacturing techniques, and were happy to start an improvement initiative that combined lean and risk management techniques straight away.

Learning By taking a critical analysis of current performance, Marieke was able to identify areas of future concern. Whilst the company was still seen to be a market leader, if she had not taken proactive action to address her future concerns, it would have lost sales to better-performing competitors. The introduction of lean techniques combined with best practice risk management tools had a dramatic impact on delivery, and now over 99 per cent of products are delivered to customers on time and within budget.

Becoming a director

What is the role of the director?

Few organisations have the formal title of chief risk officer (CRO), but most will have a member of the executive team committed to driving risk management forward. In some organisations this will be the operations director, in others it will be the finance director or in a project-oriented organisation it could be a head of programmes. Whatever the title, the senior director responsible for risk management will fulfil various roles in addition to meeting statutory responsibilities:

→ setting the overall risk management strategy and gaining the active support of the chief executive and other members of the board

→ being able to express the total risk to the business in qualitative and, where appropriate, quantitative terms

→ ensuring that risk management is appropriately utilised in winning new business and is positioned as a competitive differentiator

→ championing risk management across the channel between risk managers and the board so that sufficient budget and resources are assigned to risk management activities across the organisation in the face of competition from operating divisions and other functions

→ ensuring board members are aware of critical trends in risk management in the marketplace, the possible impact of each of these on business performance, and the implications in terms of driving fundamental change

→ designing the overall risk management framework and putting in place the appropriate teams and risk management champions to ensure effective implementation

→ reporting on risk management progress and performance to the board, conducting stakeholder presentations and briefing key opinion leaders inside and outside the organisation.

What statutory responsibilities are there?

As well as heading up the risk management activities throughout the business, you will have certain roles and statutory responsibilities that accompany the title of director. As a member of the board of directors, you will be responsible to the shareholders of the company and be involved in:

→ determining the company's strategic objectives and policies

→ monitoring progress towards achieving the objectives and policies

→ appointing the senior management team

→ accounting for the company's activities to relevant parties (e.g. shareholders)

→ ensuring you meet regulatory requirements, environmental standards and corporate social responsibilities

→ attending board meetings that run the company with the high level of integrity that is inferred by statutory standards and the company's interpretation of corporate governance, particularly in sensitive areas such as health and safety.

You will also have to conduct yourself in a highly professional manner:

→ Directors must not put themselves in a position where the interests of the company conflict with their personal interest or duty to a third party.

→ Directors must not make a personal profit out of their direct-orial position unless they are permitted to do so by the company.

→ Directors must act in a bona fide manner in what they consider to be in the interests of the company as a whole, and not for any other purpose and with no other agenda.

How do I get to the top?

Ask yourself 'Do I really want to get to the top?' In our early careers we often believe that this should be our natural goal, but for many people the price is too high. Whilst the personal and financial rewards can be high, many people do not enjoy the additional responsibilities, stress and pressures on the work–life balance that is often associated with getting to the top.

For one successful project manager, for example, an annual review with his boss was clearly not going well. Whilst he had met all his targets, his boss was telling him what he now needed to do to get himself ready for his next promotion. After a very difficult 30-minute discussion his boss simply asked him: 'Look, don't you want to get promoted?' This was followed by silence – he had never actually thought about it in this rather stark way. After some thought, he simply replied 'No!' He enjoyed the nuts and bolts of project management and really didn't want to get involved with the 'politics' of becoming an overall programme manager.

Ask yourself a couple of simple questions:

→ Can I think and act strategically, having spent my career to date in operational roles?

→ Do I understand other functions sufficiently to be able to integrate the necessary risk activities?

Take time to get to know the senior person who currently has the role that you aspire to. What do they do on a day-to-day basis, and what do they need to achieve for success? What are the pressures and the risks specific to the role? Recognise that the more senior you get the more lonely the position is, as you end up with fewer and fewer peers. It is often said that the role of the chief executive is the loneliest one in the business.

But getting to the top in any field is often rewarding and enjoyable. So if you want it go for it. Make sure you understand what criteria senior managers use to assess potential candidates for the job, and seek the opportunity to work-shadow the current incumbent. Don't leave this too late as it may take you two years or more to acquire the necessary experience and skills.

Planning your 'exit strategy'

At some stage you will want to change role. You may be moving into a different function, getting your boss's job, or simply retiring, but whatever the situation the way you manage the transition is critical to sustaining the performance of your team. This is particularly important if you are considering taking members of your team with you. Take time to plan the last ten weeks in your current role to the same level of detail as you did the first ten weeks, ensuring that your successor is well prepared and excited about taking on their new role.

What is succession planning?

As soon as you have successfully completed your first ten weeks you should start to think about who will be your natural replacement. You may want to identify two or three candidates per role, and remember that it may take at least two years to develop their skills and experience. There may be more than one internal candidate, or it may be that none will meet the criteria, but in either case your succession is important, and you need to plan it in advance.

Handover tips

At the point of transition, manage the handover to your successor effectively, ensuring that you transfer knowledge (both explicit and implicit) and relationships smoothly. Use the checklist of 'things to know' at the end of your first ten weeks as a structure for preparing your hand-over document. Then focus on people and key relationships, taking time to introduce your successor face to face rather than simply sending around an email. Take time to reflect on your original vision and how well you achieved it, then capture a list of lessons learned and add it to your hand-over notes.

EXPERT VOICE

Risk management: a business enabler

Dr Whitney van der Linde Department of Business and Management, University of Johannesburg, SA

Excessive 'risk taking' has been the blame of almost all of the financial and economic disasters that the world has encountered. But this is not only applicable to the financial sector. The majority of modern civilisation's disasters can be laid at the door of 'human induced' interventions or non-interventions – and then shifting the fundamental problem to a symptomatic problem, calling it 'risk'.

Due to pressures from stakeholders, organisations even appointed risk managers, created risk management departments, and became focussed on a 'tick' on a compliance document. The existence of a risk manager may well have less to do with actual risk reduction than it has to do with the *impression* of risk reduction. Concerns about the role along with growing stakeholder pressure is leading to a critical re-evaluation of 'risk' and 'risk management'.

The concept of risk as a modern phenomenon originated as a discipline from economic science (Adam Smith, 1723–1790) and stayed within the ambit of economic sciences for a few years, but as a discipline within a science it must also and has also evolved. The past two decades saw an exponential growth in the body of knowledge with various interpretations – which forced the international management community to look at a standardised 'risk management' body of knowledge. This body of knowledge eventually culminated in the International Standards Organisation's ISO 31000 (2009) (Risk management – Principles and guidelines), supported by Guide 73 to ISO 31000 (Risk management – Vocabulary). For the first time a uniform definition of 'risk' is accepted.

Risk is being defined as 'effect of uncertainty on objectives'. This simple yet highly effective definition provides the three main criteria for risk and risk management. Firstly, for a risk to be present there must be an objective. Without an objective there can be no risk. How does an organisation determine objectives? Organisations cannot determine objectives as an organisation is a non-rational, non-human entity: individuals (human beings) take decisions. Decisions taken by individuals cannot happen in isolation (the risk management department) as they will influence other activities within the organisation. Secondly, the achievement of this objective (as envisaged by the organisation and individual) is surrounded by uncertainty. This uncertainty (or the minimisation of this uncertainty) is influenced from within and from outside the organisation. Uncertainty within the organisation is under the control of the organisation (as presented by individuals). Uncertainty from outside the organisation is not under the control of the organisation (but against which the organisation can make contingency plans). Thirdly, the effect of this uncertainty can be positive or negative. The positive effect provides the organisation with advantages that can be exploited and these have unforeseen effects that were not envisaged. An example is the iPod, a technology advanced music player that disrupted industries, from music and telecommunications, and eventually affected knowledge sharing. A negative effect can also lead to the demise of the organisation – as the so-called 'toxic assets' had on Lehman Brothers. Risk is not the event or consequence of an activity, the risk has now been realised. The downfall of Lehman Brothers is not a risk – the risk has now materialised.

Typically an organisation will have strategic objectives, functional or tactical objectives and operational objectives. Strategic and functional objectives can only be achieved by what is happening at the operational level. The operational objectives and activities to deliver these objectives must be focused upwards towards the functional and strategic objectives. These objectives and activities at the operational level are surrounded by uncertainties. These uncertainties are influenced by a control – commonly known as standing working procedures (SOPs) or reference guides to gain control over the uncertainties that can influence the activities and thus the objectives. If the individual who performs the required activity doesn't understand how their actions can influence the outcome of that activity (either positive or negative), then that activity will not be value adding. From above it can be stated that 'risk' and 'risk management' is the responsibility of every employee and not just that of the 'strange' position of the risk manager, and/or risk management department.

The only way organisations can reap the benefit of 'risk' and 'risk management' is for all employees to know, become knowledgeable and implement risk management principles. Only then will risk management be a business enabler and not a position creating the 'perception' of risk and risk management.

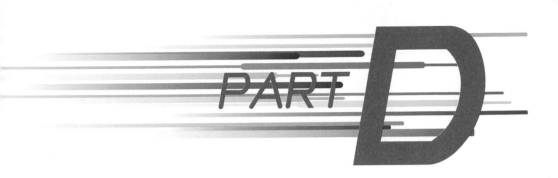

PART D

DIRECTOR'S TOOLKIT

I n Part B we introduced ten core tools and techniques that can be used from day one in your new role as a team leader or manager in your chosen field. As you progress up the career ladder to the role of senior manager, and as your team matures in terms of its understanding and capabilities, you will want to introduce more advanced and sophisticated techniques.

Part D provides a number of more advanced techniques[1] developed and adopted by industry leaders – helping you to stand out from your competitors.

	TOOL DESCRIPTION
T1	Assessing the risk management maturity of the organisation
T2	Accurately quantifying risk
T3	Using risk as a competitive differentiator
T4	Black swans – avoiding business disasters

---

[1] All tools and techniques are available online at **www.Fast-Track-Me.com**

T1 ASSESSING THE RISK MANAGEMENT MATURITY OF THE ORGANISATION

Businesses generally find it difficult to execute processes consistently across the enterprise. Even when they achieve this, how do they know that they are doing a good job relative to their competitors? This was the question that was addressed by the Software Engineering Institute in the late 1980s. By implication, the initial work was focused on improving the quality of software development and this resulted in the capability maturity model (CMM). This was developed and expanded over time into capability maturity model integration (CMMI) and broadened to cover general business processes and project management in particular. Today many organisations use CMMI to benchmark and improve overall business performance.

CMMI capability maturity levels

The basic CMMI model uses five levels of 'maturity' assessment:

1 **Initial** – Process unpredictable, poorly controlled and reactive.

2 **Repeatable** – Process standardised for individual projects and is often reactive.

3 **Defined** – Process standardised for the organisation and is proactive.

4 **Managed** – Process effectiveness measured and controlled.

5 **Optimised** – Focus on continuous process improvement.

These levels are assessed from a matrix (or set of matrices) containing statements that you compare your current organisational status with. You rate your project/business/enterprise against these statements to deduce the level of 'capability' and 'maturity' that you currently have. The catch here is that you are only as good as your lowest level of assessment (for example, you could score 4s and 5s on every area but one could be at level 1). This means that overall you are only at capability maturity level 1.

Let's look at the matrix and how you assess your maturity capability using it.

The enterprise risk management maturity matrix

The enterprise risk management maturity matrix (see figure opposite) was developed by De-RISK to address perceived limitations of the CMMI model in the area of risk management. That is to say, the CMMI model looks at risk management as one small component of project management and therefore you could fall into the trap of rating your risk management capability highly without really understanding what it takes to make risk management work effectively in your business. Therefore the enterprise risk management maturity matrix is really an expansion of CMMI specifically for risk management although it deliberately follows the CMMI rules, in a loose way, in order to provide a pragmatic and quick way of assessing risk management capability.

The areas of examination in the matrix have been selected to cover the complete business environment from top to bottom:

→ **Strategy.** Looking at how the business strategy addresses risk management and how this is reflected into relationships with clients.

→ **Team.** Covering risk management roles and responsibilities.

	1-Initial Little or no focus on risk management	2-Repeatable Individual approaches established and repeatable	3-Defined Consistent approach, shared understanding	4-Managed Measures and controls established and used	5-Optimising Focus on continuous improvement
Strategy	• Business strategy does not explicitly address risk management (RM)	• Concept of risk management (RM) built into business strategy	• Enterprise-wide RM strategy established • RM an integral part of business strategy • Joint RM strategy established with clients	• RM strategy defines measures and KPIs • RM intergrated into overall business balanced scorecard	• RM strategy documents continuous improvement measures • Continuous improvement executed systematically
Team	• Team roles and responsibilities do not address RM • Significant duplication of effort	• RM R&Rs determined by individual projects • Minimal duplication of effort	• RM R&Rs consistent across enterprise • No duplication of effort • 'Risk champions' assigned	• Team RM effectiveness is regularly measured and corrective action taken • RM effectiveness included as part of performance evaluations	• Team R&Rs include evaluation against continuous improvement • RM R&Rs regularly reviewed for potential improvement
Process	• Focus on issues rather than risks • RM process not formally documented • Driven by audit requirements only • Little planned mitigation	• RM processess established for individual projects/areas • Regular risk reviews • Coordinated with audit • Mitigations followed through	• Projects prioritised for RM • Consistent process across projects • Escalation to senior management effective • Systematic risk review • Fully integrated with audit	• Metrics collected to measure RM effectiveness as an integral part of the process	• RM process focus is on processess improvement • Process is regularly reviewed for potential improvement • Risk knowledge is captured and reused
IT	• No RM tools, or simple spreadsheets used in some areas • No policy on use of RM IT tools	• Spreadsheets or standalone databases used on each project/business area • Policy for IT support established but not fully implemented	• Common RM IT system used across enterprise • Internet-based to enable risk data sharing and escalation • Significant automation to reduce admin	• Automated exception-based risk warning indicators • Automatic escalation • Automated RM metric generation	• IT supports knowledge management and lessons learned • IT has capability to support additional metrics
Culture	• Reluctance to acknowledge risk • Informal RM based on management experience and intuition	• Individual managers have clearly embraced RM • Some formal procedures in place	• Enterprise-wide endorsement of common RM procedures • Management have clearly embraced RM • RM is approached from a positive perspective	• Management act appropriately on metrics • Top-to-bottom RM 'walk the talk' evident	• All team members feel empowered to contribute to process and tool improvements • Positive 'think risk' culture

→ **Process.** Examining the consistency and effectiveness of the risk management processes.

→ **IT.** Looking at the IT software tools used and how effective they really are at supporting and improving risk management.

→ **Culture.** Reviewing attitudes to risk and risk management across the business.

The maturity assessment process

Start on the left-hand side of the grid opposite and read the assessment under 1-Initial. This is 'worst case' and you must be at level 1 as a minimum. Now read the statements in 2–Repeatable. If you can satisfy all aspects of the statement move on to level 3 and so on. When you have assessed your business against each area, take the lowest score against any area and this is your overall level of risk management maturity. The idea is that you are only as good as your weaknesses.

You can do this assessment yourself or get it done by individual team members either privately or together in a small workshop. However, a good approach is to get individuals to do the assessment themselves before doing a workshop and use the 'worst case' across the team as your starting point. This should ensure that specific concerns are captured and discussed before consensus is reached on the appropriate level.

Improving maturity levels

It follows that improvement in overall maturity level can only be achieved by focusing on the weaker areas first and bringing everything up to a consistent level before trying to move the business to the next level overall.

Most organisations will start this process by assessing themselves to be at level 1 and a few will start at level 2. Personally, I have never come across an organisation that is at level 3 on their first assessment.

The target for most businesses is to get to level 3, as a minimum, as this gives consistency and effectiveness across the enterprise. This can take months or years to achieve, depending on the size of the organisation.

Implementing all the Fast Track top ten in Chapter 3 along with the technology recommendations of Chapter 4 and change management principles of Chapter 5 will take you directly to level 3/4 and potentially beyond.

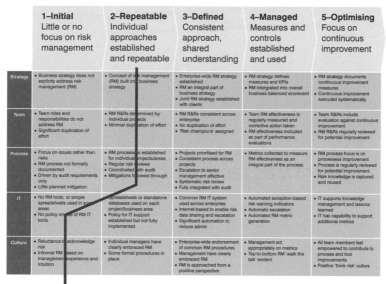

	1–Initial Little or no focus on risk management	**2–Repeatable** Individual approaches established and repeatable	**3–Defined** Consistent approach, shared understanding	**4–Managed** Measures and controls established and used	**5–Optimising** Focus on continuous improvement
Strategy	• Business strategy does not explicitly address risk management (RM)	• Concept of risk management (RM) built into business strategy	• Enterprise-wide RM strategy established • RM an integral part of business strategy • Joint RM strategy established with clients	• RM strategy defines measures and KPIs • RM intergrated into overall business balanced scorecard	• RM strategy documents continuous improvement measures • Continuous improvement executed systematically
Team	• Team roles and responsibilities do not address RM • Significant duplication of effort	• RM R&Rs determined by individual projects • Minimal duplication of effort	• RM R&Rs consistent across enterprise • No duplication of effort • 'Risk champions' assigned	• Team RM effectiveness is regularly measured and corrective action taken • RM effectiveness included as part of performance evaluations	• Team R&Rs include evaluation against continuous improvement • RM R&Rs regularly reviewed for potential improvement
Process	• Focus on issues rather than risks • RM process not formally documented • Driven by audit requirements only • Little planned mitigation	• RM processes established for individual projects/areas • Regular risk reviews • Coordinated with audit • Mitigations followed through	• Projects prioritised for RM • Consistent process across projects • Escalation to senior management effective • Systematic risk review • Fully integrated with audit	• Metrics collected to measure RM effectiveness as an integral part of the process	• RM process focus is on processess improvement • Process is regularly reviewed for potential improvement • Risk knowledge is captured and reused
IT	• No RM tools, or simple spreadsheets used in some areas • No policy on use of RM IT tools	• Spreadsheets or standalone databases used on each project/business area • Policy for IT support established but not fully implemented	• Common RM IT system used across enterprise • Internet-based to enable risk data sharing and escalation • Significant automation to reduce admin	• Automated exception-based risk warning indicators • Automatic escalation • Automated RM metric generation	• IT supports knowledge management and lessons learned • IT has capability to support additional metrics
Culture	• Reluctance to acknowledge risk • Informal RM based on management experience and intuition	• Individual managers have clearly embraced RM • Some formal procedures in place	• Enterprise-wide endorsement of common RM procedures • Management have clearly embraced RM • RM is approached from a positive perspective	• Management act appropriately on metrics • Top-to-bottom RM 'walk the talk' evident	• All team members feel empowered to contribute to process and tool improvements • Positive 'think risk' culture

▌ = Level 1

	1–Initial Little or no focus on risk management	**2–Repeatable** Individual approaches established and repeatable	**3–Defined** Consistent approach, shared understanding	**4–Managed** Measures and controls established and used	**5–Optimising** Focus on continuous improvement
Strategy	• Business strategy does not explicitly address risk management (RM)	• Concept of risk management (RM) built into business strategy	• Enterprise-wide RM strategy established • RM an integral part of business strategy • Joint RM strategy established with clients	• RM strategy defines measures and KPIs • RM intergrated into overall business balanced scorecard	• RM strategy documents continuous improvement measures • Continuous improvement executed systematically
Team	• Team roles and responsibilities do not address RM • Significant duplication of effort	• RM R&Rs determined by individual projects • Minimal duplication of effort	• RM R&Rs consistent across enterprise • No duplication of effort • 'Risk champions' assigned	• Team RM effectiveness is regularly measured and corrective action taken • RM effectiveness included as part of performance evaluations	• Team R&Rs include evaluation against continuous improvement • RM R&Rs regularly reviewed for potential improvement
Process	• Focus on issues rather than risks • RM process not formally documented • Driven by audit requirements only • Little planned mitigation	• RM processess established for individual projects/areas • Regular risk reviews • Coordinated with audit • Mitigations followed through	• Projects prioritised for RM • Consistent process across projects • Escalation to senior management effective • Systematic risk review • Fully integrated with audit	• Metrics collected to measure RM effectiveness as an integral part of the process	• RM process focus is on processess improvement • Process is regularly reviewed for potential improvement • Risk knowledge is captured and reused
IT	• No RM tools, or simple spreadsheets used in some areas • No policy on use of RM IT tools	• Spreadsheets or standalone databases used on each project/business area • Policy for IT support established but not fully implemented	• Common RM IT system used across enterprise • Internet-based to enable risk data sharing and escalation • Significant automation to reduce admin	• Automated exception-based risk warning indicators • Automatic escalation • Automated RM metric generation	• IT supports knowledge management and lessons learned • IT has capability to support additional metrics
Culture	• Reluctance to acknowledge risk • Informal RM based on management experience and intuition	• Individual managers have clearly embraced RM • Some formal procedures in place	• Enterprise-wide endorsement of common RM procedures • Management have clearly embraced RM • RM is approached from a positive perspective	• Management act appropriately on metrics • Top-to-bottom RM 'walk the talk' evident	• All team members feel empowered to contribute to process and tool improvements • Positive 'think risk' culture

▌ = Level 3

T2 ACCURATELY QUANTIFYING RISK

Applying risk management to an ongoing programme to 'rescue it' is quite a common occurrence but it is clearly not the best way to operate The problem is that the programme has already gone wrong and this is often due to the fact that the estimating assumptions made when the projects were in the scoping/proposal stage were fundamentally incorrect. This often leads to insufficient budgets, shortcuts and damaged business relationships that ultimately undermine the project, leading to delays, scoping reductions and even total project or programme failure.

So what's wrong with traditional estimating techniques?

Traditional estimating approaches take 'good quality' estimates (e.g. capital assets) and 'poor quality' estimates (e.g. resource estimates for activities never attempted before) and simply add them together to produce an 'add-up cost' which conceals the uncertainties (i.e. the risk). Further, if these uncertainties are now lost in the add-up cost, there is no way of re-analysing them and therefore no way of managing the cost risk by directly addressing the uncertainty risks.

What can be done to improve this?

Quality based costing (QBC) is a proven way of accurately estimating the cost risk in any size of programme. The term 'cost risk' in this context could be pure cost, timescale or even benefit realisation. It essentially works by capturing the inevitable quality variations in the estimates and underpins all estimates with their underlying assumptions.

So how does quality based costing work?

Quality based costing starts by first identifying the strategic cost 'bricks' in the project. The term 'brick' is used to avoid confusion with work packages, activities, tasks, etc. and the size of a brick can vary considerably depending on the stage of project. The first step is to identify all the cost bricks and therefore build the 'brick wall'. When this is complete, the total cost structure of the project is represented, with no estimates at this stage.

Brick owners are allocated for each brick based on the ability to estimate and understand the specific brick as accurately as possible. Brick owners are then interviewed to 'break down' the brick estimates into its components.

Do this by asking structured questions that break the brick down into:

A = **A**bsolute minimum (what would be the estimate if everything went perfectly?)

A+B = **B**est guess/realistic estimate (what would a single-point estimate be – with no added contingency?)

A+B+C = **C**ontingency added (what would need to be added to make the estimate 'comfortable'?)

A+B+C+D = **D**isaster scenario (is there an unlikely situation where things could go very badly wrong?)

The assumptions that underpin the estimates are also captured using the ABCD assumption analysis process as shown in Chapter 3 – see the figure opposite. The key factor here is that the ratings of the assumptions must be consistent with the estimate breakdown, and the interview often results in challenges to the estimates and/or assumptions to make them mutually consistent. One significant benefit is that inappropriate contingency will be stripped out and required contingency will be maintained or added in.

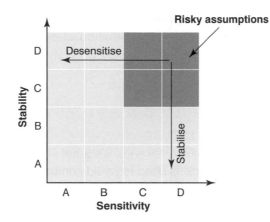

Each brick then has two probability distributions built around the estimates – one for the 'contingency scenario' and one for the 'disaster scenario', as shown in the diagram below.

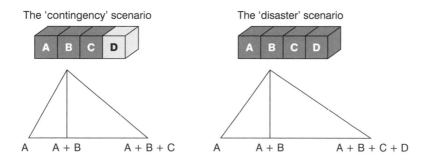

Monte Carlo analysis is a standard technique for adding together probability distributions and is therefore used to add the bricks statistically.

The resulting probability distributions – see the figure overleaf – can be interpreted to make crucial decisions relating to budgeting, pricing or milestones. For example:

→ There is a 'zero' probability of the project costing less than the 'base cost'.

→ The 50 per cent confidence cost means that there is a 50-50 chance of the project costing less or more than this value.

→ The 90 per cent confidence cost is normally considered to be the 'ideal' cost to budget (if this is considered affordable).

→ To be meaningful, the project must be funded somewhere between the 50 per cent and 90 per cent costs.

→ The add-up cost is simply the value that would have been reached through 'traditional' estimating.

→ The add-up cost could appear anywhere on the graph but experience has shown this to be consistently below the 50 per cent point – is it therefore not surprising that traditional estimating is so far out?

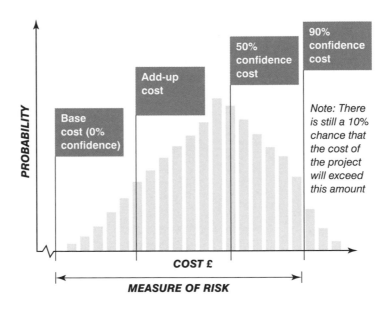

Using QBC for competitive advantage

QBC is most effectively used at the proposal stage of a project or programme to provide the best possible information for competitive pricing and to give confidence that crucial milestones will be met. In non-competitive environments, it provides a scientific way of guaranteeing fair budgets and profit. In competitive situations, it allows suppliers to understand the level of risk that they are taking on if they choose to cut their price or timescales for strategic reasons. However, it also allows for innovative pricing scenarios, which can produce the most aggressive (fixed) price but with reduced risk to the supplier:

→ Identify all bricks where a client dependency is driving the uncertainty.

→ Take out the C and D components for these bricks and rerun the simulation.

→ The difference between the profiles allows a fixed price and a 'contingency' to be negotiated.

→ Capture and quantify the value of these assumptions in the contract.

→ Rerun the simulation periodically (e.g. at each major milestone).

See the diagram below.

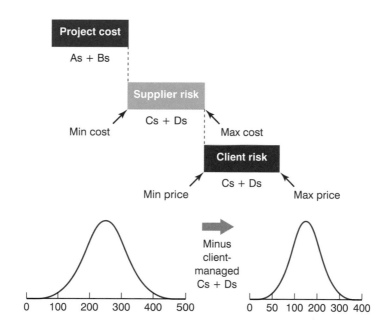

T3 USING RISK AS A COMPETITIVE DIFFERENTIATOR

Many sales professionals will shy away from the subject of risk, preferring to play down or deliberately ignore the inherent risks in their proposals. Good sales professionals will realise that risk can be turned around to become a massive competitive differentiator, and the way that risk is dealt with can be the difference between winning and losing a deal. So how can we handle such a delicate subject so that it is turned to our advantage?

Quantifying cost risks as a route to the lowest practical price

If we can accurately identify the cost risk in the deal, we will be well placed to offer the lowest competitive price and hence be in a strong position to ultimately win the deal. Unfortunately, there are significant challenges in quantifying the risks using traditional risk methods, as the numbers are little more than guesswork with little or no consistent rationale behind them. Few potential clients are going to buy into this approach and it may come over as simply a way of inflating the price.

The ABCD quality based costing (QBC) technique, as discussed in T2, is a way of modelling uncertainty in a way that ensures that the best available data is used and fully justified. It essentially works by acknowledging the inevitable quality variations in the estimates and underpins all estimates with their underlying assumptions to explain these quality variations.

Having quantified assumptions will put you in a very powerful negotiating position.

→ **Your responsibility.** Some assumptions will be your responsibility to manage and you will need to allow enough budget to either proactively manage and/or cover contingency plans. This could be done either by including the cost in your price or by taking a commercial decision to invest in order to keep the price down and win the business. Either way, you make your decision in the full knowledge of the quantified risk that you are taking. Also note that, depending on the nature of the deal, you may be able to use this analysis to justify your price by explicitly showing that your price is what it is because you need to cover specific risks.

→ **Your customer's responsibility.** Some assumptions will be the responsibility of your customer to manage. Make sure that you are not including budget to manage these assumptions or it may inflate your price inappropriately. With these figures you can engage with your customer in a very interesting discussion. Assuming that your customer agrees with your assessment of responsibility, you can be confident of the scope of your commercial offer. You have identified something valuable for your customer, as they know what budget/contingency they need to allocate to cover this risk. However, what might happen is that the customer may want you to take on some of this risk and therefore you will be able to increase your price in order to cover this.

→ **Third-party responsibility.** Similarly, you may identify some assumptions that are the responsibility of other organisations to manage. Again you are bringing something valuable to your customer and helping them to manage the commercial side of the programme more efficiently.

Possibly the main benefit of this type of analysis is that you will demonstrate to your customers that you understand their business requirements better than the competition and that will put you in a very powerful position when they are short-listing suppliers.

Guaranteeing delivery

As important as cost/price and possibly more important to the client is their confidence in your ability to deliver to agreed timescales. The client is undertaking the programme of work to gain tangible and/or intangible benefits. It is highly likely that any delays to delivery times will be eating away into these benefits, and delaying them at the very least, so anything that you do to show that you stand a higher chance of delivering on time than your competitors could be crucial in securing the deal.

Using an approach like the ABCD quality based costing approach, the timescale risk can be accurately quantified in a similar way to the cost risk. The main difference here is that the timescale 'bricks' will be the activities that lie along the critical path (i.e. the longest route through the project plan). Be aware that at the deal stage the critical path may not be obvious and there may be multiple potential critical paths that are possible due to the inevitable uncertainties at this early phase of the enterprise. The solution here is to model all potential critical paths to see which is actually the longest. There may only be two or three alternatives and I have never seen more than eight alternative critical paths in one programme plan.

The initial timescale assessment should be done as early in the proposal stage as is practical (i.e. as soon as outline plans are available – the model can be updated and run again relatively easily if the plans change). This will yield a probability distribution – see the graph overleaf – that will allow you to read off the percentage probability of achieving any given target date. It is not unusual to discover, at this stage, that the target date has a relatively low probability of being achieved. Increasing the probability is a matter of managing (or showing how to manage) the underlying assumptions. As in the cost analysis above, you can legitimately 'discount' the delays that would be due to the client and third parties. You can then show a profile that shows a high probability of delivery *if* the client and third parties meet their commitments. It may also be appropriate to show different scenarios based on whether these risks are managed effectively or not.

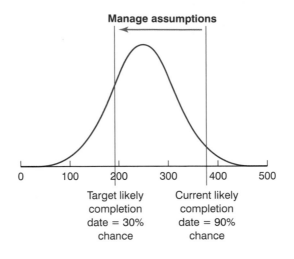

Manage assumptions

| 0 | 100 | 200 | 300 | 400 | 500 |

Target likely
completion
date = 30%
chance

Current likely
completion
date = 90%
chance

Sometimes the initial assessment shows that the target date has a '0 per cent' chance of being achieved. This means that the delivery target is impossible with the current approach and will require a differently structured plan, i.e. more activities will need to be planned in parallel. It is important to note that the estimates you are putting into this assessment are all yours, as there is unlikely to be any customer (or third-party) input at the proposal stage. This should not be a problem as it demonstrates a high degree of understanding and transparency and may open up a productive dialogue with the client. The analysis also shows the client how the timescale risk can be systematically reduced by managing the identified assumptions. It should be made clear that the analysis will be redone, jointly, following the contract award.

As in the cost analysis, the assumptions will uncover opportunities as well as risks so you may even be able to identify how you could deliver early. The competition is unlikely to have thought of that one.

Shadowing the competitor's risks

It is very common for clients to ask suppliers to identify the risks as part of the proposal. Very often this results in suppliers providing a highly sanitised risk register that only expose the risks that the supplier is comfortable to discuss. Intelligent clients realise what is going on and may penalise suppliers for not being open or not understanding their business issues.

Further, you may be aware of risks that you are well positioned to manage but you suspect that the competition is not. It is then difficult for you to highlight these risks, using traditional risk management methods, without coming over as overtly negative.

Using ABCD assumption analysis, shadowing the competitor's risks becomes a lot easier to do as you are focusing on the positive assumptions rather than the negative risks.

All the key assumptions that must happen in order to deliver the client's objectives should be listed. The assumptions should be rated honestly from your perspective and any 'at risk' should have substantive mitigation plans. For assumptions that you are confident that you have an edge over the competition, stress your strengths clearly and leave it at that.

Your assumptions will probably be used as a checklist against which the competitors' risks will be compared, and inevitably there will be 'gaps' that will seed doubt in the client's mind that the competition is either not being completely honest or do not understand the problems that the proposal is supposed to address. Either way, your standing is improved in the client's mind.

There is obviously additional cost in using the techniques described here but the return on investment should be very high. Firstly, you would only use the approaches on your most strategically important deals and, secondly, remember the difference in return between coming first and second.

T4 BLACK SWANS – AVOIDING BUSINESS DISASTERS

This book has concentrated on the proactive application of risk management. However, as a director, you will be expected to be aware of and take appropriate action to manage potential business disasters.

In 2008, Nassim Nicholas Taleb published a book called *The Black Swan*. A black swan is defined as being an event which has three characteristics: it is highly improbable, has massive impact and, in a strange way, appears almost inevitable after the event. Due, no doubt, to the timing of Taleb's book's publication relative to world events, the term 'black swan' has crept into business language. So how do we protect our businesses from black swans?

Black swan events

Taleb coined the term 'black swan' from the story of the discovery that black swans existed. Before the discovery of the New World, the Old World assumed that all swans must be white. In other words, if a black swan had never been seen, then it was assumed that the possibility of a non-white swan was so improbable as to be non-existent.

Examples of recent black swan events are 9/11, the success of Google and the recent global financial crisis. Many people would say that any or all of these examples could have been predicted, but even if some people did foresee these events, then no significant mitigating actions were taken or their impact (or success) would not have been so great.

For most growing businesses, a black swan event would be a risk that has not been explicitly considered and that would lead to a major setback for the business and even complete business failure.

So why doesn't risk management cope with black swans?

Traditional risk management relies on identifying risks based on the experience of the teams involved in the enterprise. If the risk is outside the experience of the group, it is unlikely to be considered. Even if a black swan 'risk' is considered, it is likely to be prioritised very low by being allocated an extremely low probability rating.

Risk management is not really designed to identify black swan events. Risk management concentrates of managing the risks to the enterprise that would have a significant impact and have a reasonable probability of occurring. This is simply a way of prioritising all potentially 'bad events' so that, time and resource can be allocated. It is appropriate for ongoing business operations to focus on risks in this way, but this means that, by applying traditional risk management methods, most black swan risks will not be identified and any black swan risks that are considered will be not be actioned due to their very low probability.

Brainstorming risks is highly unlikely to capture black swans. The exercise will either be too narrow, by staying within the comfort zones of the participants, or too broad by considering risks that are not relevant to your business (e.g. earthquakes in a non-earthquake zone).

In addition, the negative connotations of the word 'risk' means that people have to change the way in which they think in order to identify negative events. A much more effective way to operate is to use ABCD risk management and consider the strategic assumptions of the business, i.e. what are the things that *must* happen for your business strategy to succeed. Thinking assumptions rather than risks also helps to keep you focused on the objectives of the business and grounds any 'out there' risks in the context of your enterprise.

The assumptions are analysed for risk using sensitivity and stability – see the figure opposite. Assumptions that are rated as CC or above are considered to be 'risky assumptions'. However, up to this point, this is still a form of risk analysis and not black swan analysis.

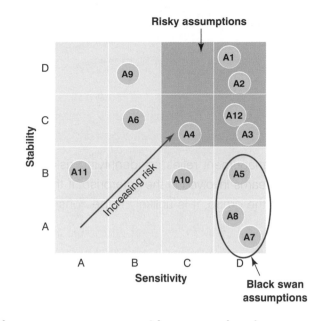

Risky assumptions

Black swan assumption analysis

So how do we use assumption analysis to identify black swans? Firstly we need to identify the strategic assumptions for our business. The strategy statement should be broken down into its constituent assumptions, i.e. the things that need to happen to ensure that the strategy is achieved. Aim for about 10–20 assumptions and ensure that you consider both internal and external factors as much as possible.

The sensitivity of the assumptions should all be rated as Cs or Ds or they are not really strategic. The stability ratings could take any rating from A to D. However, unlike risk management, it is not the CC and above rated assumptions that we are interested in – these would be handled as 'risks' and be part of the ongoing (strategic) risk management process. Black swan assumptions will be rated as sensitivity D and stability A or B, i.e. they will have a massive impact if they don't hold but are considered to be fairly or very stable.

We then need to further test the assumptions by considering relevant risk drivers in the world that could potentially affect our business strategy to a massive extent, for example:

→ market changes (e.g. oil prices, currency fluctuations, credit availability)

→ socio-political changes (e.g. change of government, adoption of Euro)

→ health crises (e.g. flu pandemic, fallout from dirty bomb).

Note that we are not looking for minor events here (e.g. oil prices rise by 10 per cent per annum) but massive events (e.g. oil prices triple in 12 months) and the compound effect of events occurring together.

We can then use these drivers to challenge the sensitivity and stability ratings and change them if appropriate. It is important to note that it may not be possible to undertake an effective assessment of risk drivers without engaging an external industry expert to challenge the internal thinking. Some limited degree of academic input or management consultant involvement may pay dividends in breaking down what Irving Janis calls 'groupthink' – i.e. the tendency for homogeneous teams to fight too hard for consensus and not to consider alternative viewpoints – and therefore miss black swans.

An effective risk driver approach will inevitably move more assumptions into the risk management category where they can be dealt with appropriately. This will leave us with a small number of assumptions that are rated as D sensitivity and A or B stability and these are our potential black swan assumptions and events.

Managing black swans

These black swan assumptions will need to be considered completely separately from the risks. By their very nature, you do not think that they will happen and therefore you will not be predisposed to take action. You basically have one choice – to desensitise your business to the effects of the assumptions – but you have two ways in which this can be accomplished, proactively or reactively.

→ **Proactive** means that you will take action now to reduce the potential impact later. This could be done by building in redundancy or standby systems, creating emergency systems, tightening procedures and so on.

→ **Reactive** would be to define contingency plans if the black swan did materialise. These may range from quite sophisticated to very basic if that is all that can be realistically done (e.g. replacing automatic systems with totally manual ones).

The highly unlikely nature of black swans will tend to lead you towards reactive rather than proactive approaches but this is not always the right thing to do. For example, think 9/11: would you rather put actions in place to deal with the situation before or after the planes had hit?

And of course the big factor is likely to be cost, but this must be weighed against the potential massive impact if the black swan materialises. In the tsunami of 2004, over 230,000 lives were lost and $15 billion of damage was done because the cost of a warning system, estimated at around $30 million, was considered too expensive. However, taking a purely narrow financial view, that works out at only $130 per life lost.

Good black swans

A final point to note is that black swans can be good as well as bad for your business. Some of the biggest business successes seemed highly unlikely but today Google and eBay are massive global businesses, the iPod (and iPad) has outsold all expectations and more recently the use of Twitter seems to be growing exponentially. Consequently, when considering your strategic assumptions, don't just look for the risks, look for investment opportunities.

THE FAST TRACK WAY

Take time to reflect

Within the Fast Track series, we cover a lot of ground quickly. Depending on your current role, company or situation, some ideas will be more relevant than others. Go back to your individual and team audits and reflect on the 'gaps' you identified, and then take time to review each of the top ten tools and techniques and list of technologies.

Next steps

Based on this review, you will identify many ideas about how to improve your performance, but look before you leap: take time to plan your next steps carefully. Rushing into action is rarely the best way to progress unless you are facing a crisis. Think carefully about your own personal career development and that of your team. Identify a starting place and consider what would have a significant impact on performance and be easy to implement. Then make a simple to-do list with timings for completion.

Staying ahead

Finally, the fact that you have taken time to read and think hard about the ideas presented suggests that you are already a professional in your chosen discipline. However, all areas of business leadership are changing rapidly and you need to take steps to stay ahead as a leader in your field. Take time to log in to the FastTrack web-resource at **www.Fast-Track-Me. com**, and join a community of like-minded professionals.

Good luck!

OTHER TITLES IN THE FAST TRACK SERIES

This title is one of many in the Fast Track series that you may be interested in exploring. Whilst each title works as a standalone solution, together they provide a comprehensive cross-functional approach that creates a common business language and structure. The series includes titles on the following:

→ Finance

→ Innovation

→ Strategy

→ Sales

→ Marketing

→ Project Management

→ Managing People & Performance

→ Managing

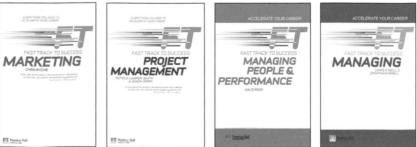

GLOSSARY

ABCD risk management A formal risk management process based on assumptions rather than risks

assumption analysis The core process of ABCD risk management that enables the identification of key assumptions and the analysis of the risk within each assumption

assumptions A description of 'what needs to happen' in order to achieve objectives expressed as 'XXX will <happen>'

assure A web-bsed toolset that fully supports the ABCD risk management process

bubble diagram A way of expressing the risk profile of a project/process by using bubbles to represent the risks

business complexity A measure of the relative complexity of the project/process measured on an ABCD scale

business criticality A measure of the importance of a project/process to the overall business measured on an ABCD scale

change programme A programme of work designed to make a significant change to the organisation

controllability A measure of the confidence that senior management have that the risky assumption can be managed, measured on an ABCD scale

credit risk The risk of loss due to a debtor's non-payment of a loan or other line of credit

criticality A measure of the overall impact of the risk to the enterprise on a Red-Amber-Green scale

enterprise A business venture – could be a project, programme, department or total business

enterprise risk management The capture, analysis and management of the total risk to the enterprise

executive sponsor The senior person who supports the project/business area and may provide representation at board level

financial risk management The practice of using financial instruments to manage exposure to risk, particularly credit risk and market risk

groupthink When groups or teams tend to take more risk than the individuals would themselves

impact The total loss (or opportunity) to the enterprise

issues Problems that exist today

market risk The risk that the value of a portfolio, either an investment portfolio or a trading portfolio, will decrease due to the change in value of the market risk factors

mitigating actions Actions taken to reduce the impact of the risk

operational risk management The process of formally managing the risk to the business operations (processes and projects)

opportunity The positive impact from an up-side risk

probability A representation (as a percentage) of the likelihood of an event occurring

process An ongoing/recurring business system

programme A set of interrelated projects that together deliver a defined business benefit programme risk management The process of managing the total risk to a programme of change

project A one-off change to the organisation

qualitative analysis The analysis (of risk) using non-numerical measures

quantitative analysis The analysis (of risk) using real (estimated) numbers

risk Potential problems (or opportunities) that may happen in the future

risk action manager The person who has the responsibility of ensuring that the risk action plans are executed

risk administrator The person responsible for the administration of the risk management process

risk assessment The process by which risks are assessed so that they can be prioritised and aggregated

risk champion The senior person who sponsors the risk management process

risk control The process by which identified risks are managed to bring them under control

risk drivers The allocation of a technical, policy or milestone category to each risk in order to look for strategic trends

risk escalation The formal process by which risks are transferred to the next level in the organisation because they cannot be managed or they have a wider impact

risk exposure The product of the risk impact and the probability

risk governance The process by which risks are formally managed as an ongoing process

risk management The formal process by which risks are proactively identified, assessed, prioritised and controlled

risk manager The traditional title for the person who is responsible for risk management in the enterprise

risk metrics A measure of the effectiveness of risk management in the organisation

risk mitigation The process of taking actions to reduce the impact of the risk

risk monitoring The ongoing process of checking the progress of risk control

risk owner The senior person who has the most interest in resolving the risk

risk plans The formal structured plan of how the risk will be managed

risk prioritisation The process of defining the appropriate order that risks should be addressed

risk review board (RRB) The senior level meeting with the remit to review and prioritise the risks, approve risk plans and monitor risk plan progress

risk screening committee (RSC) A body set up before the RRB that concentrates on ensuring the clarity of the risks and preprioritisation of the risks

risk tools Software designed to support the risk process

risk transfer The process by which the risk is reduced by passing it to a third party

risk trends The patterns in the risks that may lead to conclusions regarding underlying trends/root causes

sensitivity A measure of how much impact an assumption will have if it turns out to be wrong

stability A measure of how confident you are that the assumption will turn out to be true

strategic risk management The process by which the strategy to the organisation is formally assessed for risk

traditional risk management The basic risk management processes that have existed for many years and tend to follow the impact × probability = risk exposure formula

urgency A measure of when you need to start taking action in order to prevent the risk impacting

INDEX

Page numbers in **bold** relate to entries in the Glossary

a priori independent variable 168
ABCD risk management 12–13, 17, 19, 59, **216**
ABCD scales 47
accusations 148
action 147
add-up cost 198
administration 83–4
analysis 8
anonymous personal presence 147
antecedents 157, 158
assumption analysis 17, 36, 46, 50, 51–8, **216**
    capturing and analysing assumptions 52–8
    process 62
    process flow 57–8
assumptions 10–11, 89, **216**
    assessment for risk 54
    rating 89
    sensitivity 55–7
    stability 55–8
    testing 47
assure **216**
attitudes 152, 153
audit, risk management process 21–30
average time open risk metric 84

barriers
    to change 163–5
    removing 117
Bay of Pigs fiasco 87, 88
behaviours 152, 153
    team motivation and 157
belief, unquestioned 86
benchmarking 175
black swan
    assumption analysis 209–10
    events 207–11
    good 211
    swan management 210–11
blame-free culture 159, 161

blog 104
boring stage 163
brainstorming 7, 46
BS 31100 27, 28–9
BS 6079 30
bubble diagrams 18, 62–3, 75, 78–80, 107, **216**
budget 119
business as usual 125
business complexity 64–5, **216**
business criticality 60, 64, **216**
Business Glossary xxi
business strategy 153

call options 110
capability 176
capability maturity model integration (CMMI) 189–90
    levels 189–90
    limitations 190
capture of opportunities 91
challenge, inviting 172–4
Challenger space shuttle disaster 87–8, 89–90
change implementation 113–25
change programme **216**
change, self 151–2
Channel Tunnel 124
chief risk officer (CRO) 169, 178
claims 148
coaching 140–1, 156
collaboration, leadership style and 156
command, leadership style and 153, 156
commitment 165
communication 11–12, 138–9
communication control 148
communication plan 136
communities of practice 175
competencies 152, 153
competitive advantage, quality based costing for 198–9
competitiveness 177

competitors 172
conferences 174–5
confiscations 146
consensus driven approach to
 leadership 153, 156
consequences, team motivation and
 157–8
consultation, leadership style and 156
content 140
contingency planning 54
contingency scenario 197
contractual penalties 114
control 99
control authorities 149
controllability 60–1, **216**
cost, add-up 198
cost estimating relationships 167
cost risk 195–6
 quantifying 201–3
creativity 122
credibility 176
credit risk **216**
crime scenes 146
critical path analysis 122
criticality 60, 64, **216**
Cuban missile crisis 87, 88
culture 159
customers 172
cybercrime 147

day-to-day activities 122
deadlines 121
decision making 137
definition of risk management 5–7
delivery, guaranteeing 203–4
denial 164
denial, resistant, exploration,
 commitment (DREC) change
 model 163–5
desire 176
Digg 104
digital forensics 147
direct pressure 86
director 178–9
 role 178
 statutory responsibilities 179
disaster scenario 197
discounted free cash flow valuation
 (DCF) 109–10
documents 146

eBay 211
employees 148
Enron 87
enterprise **216**
enterprise risk management (ERM)
 7, 16, 20, 35, 36–44, 106, **216**
 benefits 37
 challenges 38–9
 implementation 43
 qualitative 40–3
 quantified 39–40
 risk prioritisation 43–4
enterprise risk management maturity
 matrix 190–2
environment, creating 159
exchange 148
executive sponsor **216**
exhibitions 174–5
exit strategy 181–2
explicit assumptions 54
explicit knowledge 181
exploration 165
external data storage 149

Facebook 104
failure of risk management 15–16
fanaticism 160
Fast-Track-Me.com xx–xxii, 175
financial impact 59, 114
financial risk management 6, 16,
 39–40, **216**
fingerprints 148
firm building 174
flexibility 121–3
forming stage 162
frame blindness 109
frequently asked questions 16–19
functional objectives 183

gambling 90
Gantt chart 118
Get2Green Action Plan xxii
GIGO (Garbage In – Garbage Out)
 38, 107
Google 207, 211
groupthink 18, 36, 85–90, 210, **216**
 ABCD and 88–9
 avoiding 88
 disasters 87–8
 symptoms 86–7

handover tips 181
HBOS 87
high/medium/low (HML) type scale
    8, 10
honeymoon period 132–3

ideas database 143
identification of risks 7
impact 8, **216**
implementation, acceleration of 91
implementation plan 117–19
implicit assumptions 54
implicit knowledge 181
indicators 6
industry advisors 172
informal review 142
informants 146
information flow 119
information sources 146–9
information suppliers 149
information technology 102
infrastructure 123–5
insurance 6
integrity 89
intelligence sources 146–9
interception 148
internal teams 172
internet 148
interrogation 146
interviews 88–9, 146
    structured 53, 54
invulnerability, illusions of 86
iPod 183, 211
ISO 31000 30, 182
issue management 13–14, 16
issues 13–15, 16, 58, **216**

joint risk management 93–5
journals 174

key opinion leaders (KOLs) 164
key performance indicators (KPIs) 143,
    169, 171, 172
knowledge 152, 153
Knowledge Cube (K-cube) xx

leadership 151–68
leadership style 153–6
learning organisation 159
Lehman Brothers 87, 183

LinkedIn 104, 174
location 146
losses 6

market risk **216**
mathematical modelling 6
maturity assessment process 192
maturity levels, improving 192–3
media 149
meetings
    one-to-one 115–16
    risk 113–15
milestones 80–2, 118
mindguards 86
mitigating actions **216**
Monte Carlo analysis 197
morality, group, unquestioned belief
    in 86
motivation, team 156–8
mourning stage 163
MyHealth Check xxi

network 146, 174
news 149
newsletters 119
norming stage 163
Northern Rock 87

observation 147
offset of risk 91
Online Coach xx–xxi
open source 148
operational directives 183
operational risk management 6, 7, 15,
    40, 42, 123–5, **216**
opportunities 19, 90–3, **216**

parametric cost analysis 166–8
partners 172
people xv, xvii
perceived risk 94
performance xiv, xvi, 169–72
    future – predictive 171
    past – historic 170
    present – current situation 171
performing stage 163
personal attributes 152–3
pharmaceutical R&D 166–8
physical material 148
plan do-check-act (PDCA) cycle 120–1

planning meeting 113–15
planning xv, xvi, 115–19
platform xv, xvi–xvii
policing cooperation 148–9
policy risk 80–2
positive approaches to risk
    management 36
positive behaviour 85
presentations 137–8
pressure, direct 86
prioritisation xv, xvi, 8, 36, 59–66
    project 17, 63–5
    risk 17, 59–61
prioritisation matrix 65
proactive management 210
probability 8, 59, **216**
probability distribution 203
process xv, xvi, 140, **216**
professional bodies 175
programme 63, **216**
programme risk management 7, 40, 42,
    76, **217**
project **217**
project prioritisation 63–5
project risk management 7, 42, 76, 123
promotion 176–7, 180
provocation 147
put options 110

qualitative analysis 10, **217**
qualitative enterprise risk management
    40–3
quality based costing (QBC) 195–9,
    201, 203
    for competitive advantage 198–9
quality, leadership style and 155
quantified enterprise risk management
    39–40
quantitative analysis 10, **217**
question, leadership style and 156
quick wins 119

Railtrack 97
RBS 87
reactive management 210
real risk 94
Red, Amber, Green (RAG) scale xxi,
    21, 43–4
relationships 177
reputation 174

reputational impact 114
reputational risk 6
resistance 164
resources 119
responsibility
    customer's 202
    personal 202
    third party 202–3
review 140
rewards 85, 161
risk action 84
risk action manager (RAM) 72, **217**
risk actions, overdue 84–5
risk administration 18, **217**
risk administrator 18, 73
risk assessment **217**
risk champion 139, **217**
risk control 68–9, **217**
risk database 105
risk, definition 96–8, 182–3, **217**
risk drivers 80–3, **217**
risk escalation 48–9, 70–1, 76, 114, **217**
risk exposure 8, **217**
risk governance 17, 36, 66–71, **217**
risk identification 114, 138–9, 141, 159
risk management
    definition **217**
    planning 8
    positive approaches 90–6
    roles 17
    standards 27–30
risk management maturity model 113
risk manager 18, 19–20, **217**
risk meetings 113–15
risk metrics 84, **217**
    behaviour and 36, 83–5
risk mitigation 8, **217**
risk monitoring 8, **217**
risk owner 72, 114, **217**
risk plan 17, 58, **217**
    objectives 69
    structuring 70
risk prioritisation 59–61, 114, **217**
risk profiles 62–3
risk registers 67, 103
risk resolution 8
risk review board (RRB) 18, 73–6,
    139–40, 142, 158, **217**
    after 75–6
    alternative structures 77

risk review board (RRB) (*continued*)
  during 75
  frequency 74
  hierarchical 76
  membership 74
  prior to meeting 74–5
risk roles and responsibilities 36, 71–8
risk screening committee (RSC)
  76, 77, **217**
risk statements 9–10, 139
risk tools **217**
risk transfer **217**
risk trends 36, 78–83, **217**
role change 131–49
  checklist 144–5
  critical time 131–2
  first ten weeks 133–43
    before starting 133–4
    week 1: getting to know
      stakeholders 135–7
    week 2: decision making, tools
      and action 137
    week 3: selling process and tool
      to wider business 137–8
    week 4: start risk identification
      138–9
    week 5: risk review board 139–40
    week 6: coach risk planning
      140–1
    week 7: second round of risk
      identification 141
    week 8: second risk review board
      142
    week 9: reflect and learn 142–5
    week 10: two-year plan 143
  potential pitfalls 132
  worst-case scenario 132–3
routines 121

scenario analysis 6
scenario planning 109–10
sceptics, converting 165
scope creep 117
securitisation 19–20
self-assessment 23, 152
self-censorship 86
self-development 173–4
self-perception 151–2
selling risk management 93
sensibility/stability scatter diagram 47–8
sensitivity 55–7, **217**

September 11th, 207, 211
shadowing risks 204–5
'six hats' (de Bono) 161
six 'Ps' xv–xvi
social media 104
spreadsheets 103, 114
stability **217**
stakeholders 135–7
standing working procedures (SOPs)
  183
stereotyping 86
stochastic algorithms 167
stop–go decision 167
storming stage 162
strategic objectives 183
strategic risk management 16, 35, 40,
  41, 45–51, **217**
stress testing 6
structured interviews 53
StumbleUpon 104
succession planning 181
supply chain 172
surveillance 147
SWOT analysis 136, 153

tactical objectives 183
team assessment 21–30
team building 160–5
team engagement 91
team training 137
technical risk 80–3
technology
  activities and choice 100–2
  appropriate 105
  availability 102–3
  process-system link 102
  reason for considering 99
  top 102–9
time 59–60
  leadership style and 154–5
  management 13, 101
time open risk metric 84
time out, taking 134
top-to-bottom integrity 89
toxic assets 183
trade magazines 174
traditional estimation techniques 195
traditional risk management 7–8, **218**
  failure 15–16
  problems with 9–10

training, team 137
transformation risk management 42
Twitter 104, 174, 211
two-year plan 143

unanimity, illusions of 86
uncertainty 182–3
urgency 61, **218**

values, shared 160–1
video cameras 147
visibility 99

web 174
web-based tool 104, 105–7
   balance 108–9
   complexity 105–6
   dashboards 107
   escalation 106
   flexibility 106
   process 107
   reports 106
   scalability 106
   security 105
   triggers 107
workshops 7, 53–4, 88, 121